ALL
THE LOVE POEMS OF
SHAKESPEARE

ALL
THE
LOVE
POEMS
OF
SHAKE-
SPEARE

DECORATIONS BY

ERIC GILL

CITADEL PRESS   SECAUCUS, N.J.

CONTENTS

VENUS & ADONIS

VENUS
AND ADONIS

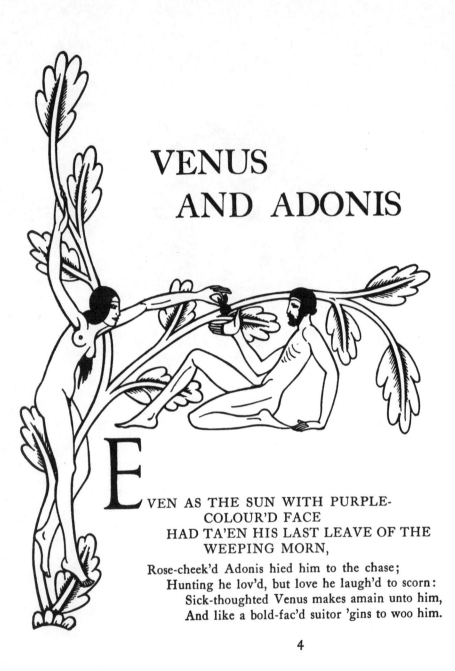

EVEN AS THE SUN WITH PURPLE-
COLOUR'D FACE
HAD TA'EN HIS LAST LEAVE OF THE
WEEPING MORN,
Rose-cheek'd Adonis hied him to the chase;
Hunting he lov'd, but love he laugh'd to scorn:
Sick-thoughted Venus makes amain unto him,
And like a bold-fac'd suitor 'gins to woo him.

"Thrice fairer than myself," thus she began,
　"The field's chief flower, sweet above compare,
"Stain to all nymphs, more lovely than a man,
　"More white and red than doves or roses are;
　　"Nature that made thee, with herself at strife,
　　"Saith that the world hath ending with thy life.

"Vouchsafe, thou wonder, to alight thy steed,
　"And rein his proud head to the saddle-bow;
"If thou wilt deign this favour, for thy meed,
　"A thousand honey-secrets shalt thou know:
　　"Here come and sit, where never serpent hisses,
　　"And being set, I'll smother thee with kisses:

"And yet not cloy thy lips with loath'd satiety,
　"But rather famish them amid their plenty
"Making them red and pale with fresh variety,
　"Ten kisses short as one, one long as twenty:
　　"A summer's day will seem an hour but short,
　　"Being wasted in such time-beguiling sport."

With this, she seizeth on his sweating palm,
　The precedent of pith and livelihood,
And, trembling in her passion, calls it balm,
　Earth's sovereign salve to do a goddess good
　　"Being wasted in such time-beguiling sport."
　　Courageously to pluck him from his horse.

Over one arm the lusty courser's rein,
　Under her other was the tender boy,
Who blush'd and pouted in a dull disdain,
　With leaden appetite, unapt to toy;
　　She red and hot, as coals of glowing fire,
　　He red for shame, but frosty in desire.

5

The studded bridle on a ragged bough
    Nimbly she fastens; (O how quick is love!)
The steed is stalled up, and even now
    To tie the rider she begins to prove:
        Backward she push'd him, as she would be
            thrust,
        And governed him in strength, though not in lust.

So soon was she along, as he was down,
    Each leaning on their elbows and their hips:
Now doth she stroke his cheek, now doth he frown,
    And 'gins to chide, but soon she stops his lips;
        And kissing speaks, with lustful language
            broken,
        "If thou wilt chide, thy lips shall never open."

He burns with bashful shame; she with her tears
    Doth quench the maiden burning of his cheeks:
Then with her windy sighs, and golden hairs,
    To fan and blow them dry again she seeks:
        He saith, she is immodest, blames her 'miss;
        What follows more, she murders with a kiss.

Even as an empty eagle, sharp by fast,
    Tires with her beak on feathers, flesh, and bone,
Shaking her wings, devouring all in haste,
    Till either gorge be stuff'd, or prey be gone;
        Even so she kiss'd his brow, his cheek, his chin,
        And where she ends, she doth anew begin.

Forc'd to content, but never to obey,
    Panting he lies, and breatheth in her face;
She feedeth on the steam, as on a prey,
    And calls it heavenly moisture, air of grace,
        Wishing her cheeks were gardens full of flowers,
        So they were dew'd with such distilling showers.

Look how a bird lies tangled in a net,
    So fasten'd in her arms Adonis lies;
Pure shame and aw'd resistance made him fret,
        Which bred more beauty in his angry eyes:
            Rain added to a river that is rank,
            Perforce will force it overflow the bank.

Still she entreats, and prettily entreats,
    For to a pretty ear she tunes her tale;
Still is he sullen, still he lowers and frets,
        'Twixt crimson shame, and anger ashy-pale;
            Being red, she loves him best; and being white,
            Her best is better'd with a more delight.

Look how he can, she cannot choose but love;
    And by her fair immortal hand she swears
From his soft bosom never to remove,
        Till he take truce with her contending tears,
            Which long have rain'd, making her cheeks all
                wet;
            And one sweet kiss shall pay this countless debt.

Upon this promise did he raise his chin,
    Like a dive-dapper peering through a wave,
Who being look'd on, ducks as quickly in;
        So offers he to give what she did crave;
            But when her lips were ready for his pay,
            He winks, and turns his lips another way.

Never did passenger in summer's heat
    More thirst for drink, than she for this good turn:
Her help she sees, but help she cannot get;
        She bathes in water, yet her fire must burn:
            "Oh, pity," 'gan she cry, "flint-hearted boy!
            " 'Tis but a kiss I beg; why art thou coy?

"I have been woo'd, as I entreat thee now,
"Even by the stern and direful god of war,
"Whose sinewy neck in battle ne'er did bow,
"Who conquers where he comes, in every jar;
"Yet hath he been my captive and my slave,
"And begg'd for that which thou unask'd shalt have.

"Over my altars hath he hung his lance,
"His batter'd shield, his uncontrolled crest,
"And for my sake hath learn'd to sport and dance,
"To toy, to wanton, dally, smile, and jest;
"Scorning his churlish drum, and ensign red,
"Making my arms his field, his tent my bed.

"Thus he that over-rul'd, I oversway'd,
"Leading him prisoner in a red-rose chain:
"Strong-temper'd steel his stronger strength obey'd,
"Yet was he servile to my coy disdain.
"O be not proud, nor brag not of thy might,
"For mastering her that foil'd the god of fight!

"Touch but my lips with those fair lips of thine,
"(Though mine be not so fair, yet are they red,)
"The kiss shall be thine own as well as mine:—
"What seest thou in the ground? hold up thy head.
"Look in mine eyeballs, there thy beauty lies:
"Then why not lips on lips, since eyes in eyes?

"Art thou asham'd to kiss? then wink again,
"And I will wink, so shall the day seem night;
"Love keeps his revels where there are but twain;
"Be bold to play, our sport is not in sight:
"These blue-vein'd violets whereon we lean
"Never can blab, nor know not what we mean.

"The tender spring upon thy tempting lip
  "Shows thee unripe; yet may'st thou well be tasted;
"Make use of time, let not advantage slip;
  "Beauty within itself should not be wasted:
    "Fair flowers that are not gather'd in their prime,
    "Rot and consume themselves in little time.

"Were I hard-favour'd, foul, or wrinkled-old,
  "Ill-nurtur'd, crooked, churlish, harsh in voice,
"O'er-worn, despised, rheumatick and cold,
  "Thick-sighted, barren, lean, and lacking juice,
    "Then might'st thou pause, for then I were not
        for thee;
    "But having no defects, why dost abhor me?

"Thou canst not see one wrinkle in my brow;
  "Mine eyes are grey, and bright, and quick in turning;
"My beauty as the spring doth yearly grow,
  "My flesh is soft and plump, my marrow burning;
    "My smooth moist hand, were it with thy hand
        felt,
    "Would in thy palm dissolve, or seem to melt.

"Bid me discourse, I will enchant thine ear,
  "Or, like a fairy, trip upon the green,
"Or, like a nymph, with long dishevell'd hair,
  "Dance on the sands, and yet no footing seen:
    "Love is a spirit all compact of fire,
    "Not gross to sink, but light, and will aspire.

"Witness this primrose bank whereon I lie;
  "These forceless flowers like sturdy trees support me;
"Two strengthless doves will draw me through the sky,
  "From morn to night, even where I list to sport me:
    "Is love so light, sweet boy, and may it be
    "That thou should'st think it heavy unto thee?

9

"Is thine own heart to thine own face affected?
  "Can thy right hand seize love upon thy left?
"Then woo thyself, be of thyself rejected,
    "Steal thine own freedom, and complain on theft.
      "Narcissus, so, himself himself forsook,
      "And died to kiss his shadow in the brook.

"Torches are made to light, jewels to wear,
    "Dainties to taste, fresh beauty for the use,
"Herbs for their smell, and sappy plants to bear;
    "Things growing to themselves are growth's abuse:
      "Seeds spring from seeds, and beauty breedeth
          beauty,
      "Thou wast begot,—to get it is thy duty.

"Upon the earth's increase why should'st thou feed,
    "Unless the earth with thy increase be fed?
"By law of Nature thou art bound to breed,
    "That thine may live, when thou thyself art dead;
      "And so in spite of death thou dost survive,
      "In that thy likeness still is left alive."

By this, the love-sick queen began to sweat,
    For, where they lay, the shadow had forsook them,
And Titan, 'tired in the midday heat,
    With burning eye did hotly overlook them;
      Wishing Adonis had his team to guide,
      So he were like him, and by Venus' side.

And now Adonis, with a lazy spright,
    And with a heavy, dark, disliking eye,
His lowering brows o'erwhelming his fair sight,
    Like misty vapours, when they blot the sky,
      Souring his cheeks, cries, "Fie, no more of love!
      "The sun doth burn my face; I must remove."

10

"Ah me," quoth Venus, "young, and so unkind!
  "What bare excuses mak'st thou to begone!
"I'll sigh celestial breath, whose gentle wind
  "Shall cool the heat of this descending sun;
    "I'll make a shadow for thee of my hairs;
    "If they burn too, I'll quench them with my tears.

"The sun that shines from heaven shines but warm,
  "And lo, I lie between that sun and thee;
"The heat I have from thence doth little harm,
  "Thine eye darts forth the fire that burneth me:
    "And were I not immortal, life were done,
    "Between this heavenly and earthly sun.

"Art thou obdurate, flinty, hard as steel,
  "Nay, more than flint, for stone at rain relenteth?
"Art thou a woman's son, and canst not feel
  "What 'tis to love? how want of love tormenteth?
    "O had thy mother borne so hard a mind,
    "She had not brought forth thee, but died
      unkind.

"What am I, that thou should'st contemn me this?
  "Or what great danger dwells upon my suit?
"What were thy lips the worse for one poor kiss?
  "Speak, fair; but speak fair words, or else be mute:
    "Give me one kiss, I'll give it thee again,
    "And one for interest, if thou wilt have twain.

"Fie, lifeless picture, cold and senseless stone,
  "Well-painted idol, image, dull and dead,
"Statue, contenting but the eye alone,
  "Thing like a man, but of no woman bred;
    "Thou art no man, though of a man's complexion,
    "For men will kiss even by their own direction."

11

This said, impatience chokes her pleading tongue
  And swelling passion doth provoke a pause;
Red cheeks and fiery eyes blaze forth her wrong;
    Being judge in love, she cannot right her cause:
      And now she weeps, and now she fain would
        speak,
      And now her sobs do her intendments break.

Sometimes she shakes her head, and then his hand,
  Now gazeth she on him, now on the ground;
Sometimes her arms infold him like a band;
    She would, he will not in her arms be bound;
      And when from thence he struggles to be gone,
      She locks her lily fingers, one in one.

"Fondling," she saith, "since I have hemm'd thee here
  "Within the circuit of this ivory pale,
"I'll be a park, and thou shalt be my deer;
    "Feed where thou wilt, on mountain or in dale:
      "Graze on my lips; and if those hills be dry
      "Stray lower, where the pleasant fountains lie.

"Within this limit is relief enough,
  "Sweet bottom-grass, and high delightful plain,
"Round rising hillocks, brakes obscure and rough,
    "To shelter thee from tempest and from rain;
      "Then be my deer, since I am such a park;
      "No dog shall rouse thee, tho' a thousand bark."

At this Adonis smiles, as in disdain,
  That in each cheek appears a pretty dimple:
Love made those hollows, if himself were slain,
    He might be buried in a tomb so simple;
      Fore-knowing well, if there he came to lie,
      Why there love liv'd, and there he could not die.

These lovely caves, these round-enchanting pits,
　　Open'd their mouths to swallow Venus' liking:
Being mad before, how doth she now for wits?
　　　Struck dead at first, what needs a second striking?
　　　　Poor queen of love, in thine own law forlorn,
　　　　To love a cheek that smiles at thee in scorn!

Now which way shall she turn? what shall she say?
　　Her words are done, her woes the more increasing,
The time is spent, her object will away,
　　　And from her twining arms doth urge releasing:
　　　　"Pity"—she cries,—"some favour—some
　　　　　remorse—"
　　　　Away he springs, and hasteth to his horse.

But lo, from forth a copse that neighbours by,
　　A breeding jennet, lusty, young, and proud,
Adonis' trampling courser doth espy,
　　　And forth she rushes, snorts, and neighs aloud:
　　　　The strong-neck'd steed, being tied unto a tree,
　　　　Breaketh his rein, and to her straight goes he.

Imperiously he leaps, he neighs, he bounds,
　　And now his woven girths he breaks asunder;
The bearing earth with his hard hoof he wounds,
　　　Whose hollow womb resounds like heaven's thunder;
　　　　The iron bit he crushes 'tween his teeth,
　　　　Controlling what he was controlled with.

His ears up prick'd; his braided hanging mane
　　Upon his compass'd crest now stand on end;.
His nostrils drink the air, and forth again,
　　　As from a furnace, vapours doth he send:
　　　　His eye, which scornfully glisters like fire,
　　　　Shows his hot courage and his high desire.

13

Sometime he trots, as if he told the steps,
　With gentle majesty, and modest pride;
Anon he rears upright, curvets and leaps,
　　As who should say, lo! thus my strength is tried;
　　　And this I do to captivate the eye
　　　Of the fair breeder that is standing by.

What recketh he his rider's angry stir,
　His flattering holla, or his *Stand, I say?*
What cares he now for curb, or pricking spur?
　　For rich caparisons, or trapping gay?
　　　He sees his love, and nothing else he sees,
　　　Nor nothing else with his proud sight agrees.

Look, when a painter would surpass the life,
　In limning out a well-proportion'd steed,
His art with nature's workmanship at strife,
　　As if the dead the living should exceed;
　　　So did this horse excell a common one,
　　　In shape, in courage, colour, pace, and bone.

Round-hoof'd, short-jointed, fetlocks shag and long,
　Broad breast, full eye, small head, and nostril wide,
High crest, short ears, straight legs, and passing strong,
　　Thin mane, thick tail, broad buttock, tender hide:
　　　Look what a horse should have, he did not lack,
　　　Save a proud rider on so proud a back.

Sometime he scuds far off, and there he stares;
　Anon he starts at stirring of a feather;
To bid the wind a base he now prepares,
　　And whether he run, or fly, they knew not whether;
　　　For thro' his mane and tail the high wind sings,
　　　Fanning the hairs, who wave like feather'd
　　　　wings.

14

He looks upon his love, and neighs unto her;
 She answers him, as if she knew his mind:
Being proud, as females are, to see him woo her,
  She puts on outward strangeness, seems unkind;
   Spurns at his love, and scorns the heat he feels,
   Beating his kind embracements with her heels.

Then, like a melancholy male-content,
 He vails his tail, that like a falling plume,
Cool shadow to his melting buttock lent;
  He stamps, and bites the poor flies in his fume:
   His love perceiveth how he is enrag'd,
   Grew kinder, and his fury was assuag'd.

His testy master goeth about to take him;
 When lo, the unback'd breeder, full of fear,
Jealous of catching, swiftly doth forsake him,
  With her the horse, and left Adonis there:
   As they were mad, unto the wood they hie them,
   Out-stripping crows that strive to over-fly them.

All swoln with chasing, down Adonis sits,
 Banning his boisterous and unruly beast;
And now the happy season once more fits,
  That love-sick Love by pleading may be blest;
   For lovers say, the heart hath treble wrong,
   When it is barr'd the aidance of the tongue.

An oven that is stopp'd, or river stay'd,
 Burneth more hotly, swelleth with more rage:
So of concealed sorrow may be said;
  Free vent of words love's fire doth assuage;
   But when the heart's attorney once is mute,
   The client breaks, as desperate in his suit.

15

He sees her coming, and begins to glow,
(Even as a dying coal revives with wind),
And with his bonnet hides his angry brow;
Looks on the dull earth with disturbed mind;
Taking no notice that she is so nigh,
For all askaunce he holds her in his eye.

O what a sight it was, wistly to view
How she came stealing to the wayward boy!
To note the fighting conflict of her hue!
How white and red each other did destroy;
But now, her cheek was pale, and by and by
It flash'd forth fire, as lightning from the sky.

Now was she just before him as he sat,
And like a lowly lover down she kneels;
With one fair hand she heaveth up his hat,
Her other tender hand his fair cheek feels:
His tenderer cheek receives her soft hand's print,
As apt as new fallen snow takes any dint.

O what a war of looks was then between them!
Her eyes, petitioners, to his eyes suing;
His eyes saw her eyes as they had not seen them;
Her eyes woo'd still, his eyes disdain'd the wooing:
And all this dumb play had his acts made plain
With tears, which, chorus-like, her eyes did rain.

Full gently now she takes him by the hand,
A lily prison'd in a gaol of snow,
Or ivory in an alabaster band;
So white a friend engirts so white a foe:
This beauteous combat, wilful and unwilling,
Show'd like two silver doves that sit a billing.

Once more the engine of her thoughts began:
  "O fairest mover on this mortal round,
"Would thou wert as I am, and I a man,
    "My heart all whole as thine, thy heart my wound;
      "For one sweet look thy help I would assure thee,
      "Though nothing but my body's bane would
        cure thee."

"Give me my hand," saith he, "why dost thou feel it?"
  "Give me my heart," saith she, "and thou shalt
    have it;
"O give it me, lest thy hard heart do steel it,
    "And being steel'd, soft sighs can never grave it:
      "Then love's deep groans I never shall regard,
      "Because Adonis' heart hath made mine hard."

"For shame," he cries, "let go, and let me go;
  "My day's delight is past, my horse is gone,
"And 'tis your fault I am bereft him so;
    "I pray you hence, and leave me here alone:
      "For all my mind, my thought, my busy care,
      "Is how to get my palfrey from the mare."

Thus she replies: "Thy palfrey, as he should,
  "Welcomes the warm approach of sweet desire.
"Affection is a coal that must be cool'd;
    "Else, suffer'd, it will set the heart on fire:
      "The sea hath bounds, but deep desire hath none,
      "Therefore no marvel though thy horse be gone.

"How like a jade he stood, tied to the tree,
  "Servilely master'd with a leathern rein!
"But when he saw his love, his youth's fair fee,
    "He held such petty bondage in disdain;
      "Throwing the base thong from his bending crest,
      "Enfranchising his mouth, his back, his breast.

"Who sees his true love in her naked bed,
  "Teaching the sheets a whiter hue than white,
"But, when his glutton eye so full hath fed,
  "His other agents aim at like delight?
    "Who is so faint, that dare not be so bold,
    "To touch the fire, the weather being cold?

"Let me excuse thy courser, gentle boy;
  "And learn of him, I heartily beseech thee,
"To take advantage on presented joy;
  "Though I were dumb, yet his proceedings teach
    thee.
    "O learn to love; the lesson is but plain,
    "And, once made perfect, never lost again."

"I know not love," quoth he, "nor will now know it,
  "Unless it be a boar, and then I chase it;
" 'Tis much to borrow, and I will not owe it;
  "My love to love is love but to disgrace it;
    "For I have heard it is a life in death,
    "That laughs, and weeps, and all but with a
    breath.

"Who wears a garment shapeless and unfinish'd?
  "Who plucks the bud before one leaf put forth?
"If springing things be any jot diminish'd,
  "They wither in their prime, prove nothing worth:
    "The colt that's back'd and burthen'd being
    young,
    "Loseth his pride, and never waxeth strong.

"You hurt my hand with wringing; let us part,
  "And leave this idle theme, this bootless chat:
"Remove your siege from my unyielding heart;
  "To love's alarm it will not ope the gate.

18

"Dismiss your vows, your feigned tears, your
flattery;
"For where a heart is hard, they make no
battery."

"What! canst thou talk," quoth she, "hast thou a
tongue?
"O would thou hadst not, or I had no hearing!
"Thy mermaid's voice hath done me double wrong;
"I had my load before, now press'd with bearing:
"Melodious discord, heavenly tune harsh
sounding,
"Ear's deep-sweet music, and heart's deep-sore
wounding.

"Had I no eyes, but ears, my ears would love
"That inward beauty and invisible;
"Or, were I deaf, thy outward parts would move
"Each part in me that were but sensible:
"Though neither eyes nor ears, to hear nor see,
"Yet should I be in love, by touching thee.

"Say, that the sense of feeling were bereft me,
"And that I could not see, nor hear, nor touch,
"And nothing but the very smell were left me,
"Yet would my love to thee be still as much;
"For from the still'tory of thy face excelling
"Comes breath perfum'd, that breedeth love
by smelling.

"But O, what banquet wert thou to the taste,
"Being nurse and feeder of the other four!
"Would they not wish the feast might ever last,
"And bid Suspicion double-lock the door?
"Lest jealousy, that sour unwelcome guest,
"Should, by his stealing in, disturb the feast."

19

Once more the ruby-colour'd portal open'd,
　　Which to his speech did honey passage yield;
Like a red morn, that ever yet betoken'd
　　Wreck to the seaman, tempest to the field,
　　　　Sorrow to shepherds, woe unto the birds,
　　　　Gusts and foul flaws to herdmen and to herds.

This ill presage advisedly she marketh:
　　Even as the wind is hush'd before it raineth,
Or as the wolf doth grin before he barketh,
　　Or as the berry breaks before it staineth,
　　　　Or like the deadly bullet of a gun,
　　　　His meaning struck her ere his words begun.

And at his look she flatly falleth down,
　　For looks kill love, and love by looks reviveth:
A smile recures the wounding of a frown,
　　But blessed bankrupt, that by love so thriveth!
　　　　The silly boy believing she is dead,
　　　　Claps her pale cheek, till clapping makes it red;

And all-amaz'd brake off his late intent,
　　For sharply he did think to reprehend her,
Which cunning love did wittily prevent:
　　Fair fall the wit that can so well defend her!
　　　　For on the grass she lies as she were slain,
　　　　Till his breath breatheth life in her again.

He wrings her nose, he strikes her on the cheeks,
　　He bends her fingers, holds her pulses hard;
He chafes her lips, a thousand ways he seeks
　　To mend the hurt that his unkindness marr'd;
　　　　He kisses her; and she, by her good will,
　　　　Will never rise, so he will kiss her still.

20

The night of sorrow now is turn'd to day:
    Her two blue windows faintly she up-heaveth,
Like the fair sun, when in his fresh array
    He cheers the morn, and all the world relieveth:
        And as the bright sun glorifies the sky,
        So is her face illumin'd with her eye;

Whose beams upon his hairless face are fix'd,
    As if from thence they borrow'd all their shine.
Were never four such lamps together mix'd,
    Had not his clouded with his brows' repine;
        But hers, which thro' the crystal tears gave light,
        Shone like the moon in water seen by night.

"O, where am I," quoth she? "in earth or heaven,
    "Or in the ocean drench'd, or in the fire?
"What hour is this? or morn or weary even?
    "Do I delight to die, or life desire?
        "But now I liv'd, and life was death's annoy;
        "But now I died, and death was lively joy.

"O thou didst kill me;—kill me once again:
    "Thy eyes' shrewd tutor, that hard heart of thine,
"Hath taught them scornful tricks, and such disdain,
    "That they have murder'd this poor heart of mine;
        "And these mine eyes, true leaders to their queen,
        "But for thy piteous lips no more had seen.

"Long may they kiss each other, for this cure!
    "O never let their crimson liveries wear!
"And as they last, their verdure still endure,
    "To drive infection from the dangerous year!
        "That the star-gazers, having writ on death,
        "May say, the plague is banish'd by thy breath.

"Pure lips, sweet seals in my soft lips imprinted,
  "What bargains may I make, still to be sealing?
"To sell myself I can be well contented,
  "So thou wilt buy, and pay, and use good dealing;
    "Which purchase if thou make, for fear of slips,
    "Set thy seal-manual on my wax-red lips.

"A thousand kisses buys my heart from me;
  "And pay them at thy leisure, one by one.
"What is ten hundred touches unto thee?
  "Are they not quickly told, and quickly gone?
    "Say, for non-payment that the debt should
      double,
    "Is twenty hundred kisses such a trouble?"

"Fair queen," quoth he, "if any love you owe me,
  "Measure my strangeness with my unripe years;
"Before I know myself, seek not to know me;
  "No fisher but the ungrown fry forbears:
    "The mellow plum doth fall, the green sticks
      fast,
    "Or being early pluck'd, is sour to taste.

"Look, the world's comforter, with weary gait,
  "His day's hot task hath ended in the west:
"The owl, night's herald, shrieks, 'tis very late;
  "The sheep are gone to fold, birds to their nest;
    "And coal-black clouds that shadow heaven's
      light
    "Do summon us to part, and bid good night.

"Now let me say *good night,* and so say you;
  "If you will say so, you shall have a kiss."
"*Good night,*" quoth she; and, ere he says *adieu,*
  The honey fee of parting tender'd is:

Her arms do lend his neck a sweet embrace:
Incorporate then they seem; face grows to face.

Till, breathless, he disjoin'd, and backward drew
  The heavenly moisture, that sweet coral mouth,
Whose precious taste her thirsty lips well knew,
    Whereon they surfeit, yet complain on drouth:
      He with her plenty press'd, she faint with
        dearth,
      (Their lips together glu'd,) fall to the earth.

Now quick Desire hath caught the yielding prey,
  And glutton-like she feeds, yet never filleth;
Her lips are conquerors, his lips obey,
    Paying what ransom the insulter willeth;
      Whose vulture thought doth pitch the price so
        high,
      That she will draw his lips' rich treasure dry.

And having felt the sweetness of the spoil,
  With blindfold fury she begins to forage;
Her face doth reek and smoke, her blood doth boil,
    And careless lust stirs up a desperate courage;
      Planting oblivion, beating reason back,
      Forgetting shame's pure blush, and honour's
        wrack.

Hot, faint, and weary, with her hard embracing,
  Like a wild bird being tam'd with too much
      handling,
Or as the fleet-foot roe, that's tir'd with chasing,
    Or like the froward infant, still'd with dandling,
      He now obeys, and now no more resisteth
      While she takes all she can, not all she listeth.

What wax so frozen but dissolves with tempering,
    And yields at last to every light impression?
Things out of hope are compass'd oft with venturing,
    Chiefly in love, whose leave exceeds commission:
        Affection faints not like a pale-fac'd coward,
        But then woos best, when most his choice is
            froward.

When he did frown, O, had she then gave over,
    Such nectar from his lips she had not suck'd.
Foul words and frowns must not repel a lover;
    What though the rose have prickles? yet 'tis
           pluck'd:
        Were beauty under twenty locks kept fast,
        Yet love breaks through, and picks them all at
           last.

For pity now she can no more detain him;
    The poor fool prays her that he may depart:
She is resolv'd no longer to restrain him;
    Bids him farewell, and look well to her heart,
        The which, by Cupid's bow she doth protest,
        He carries thence incaged in his breast.

"Sweet boy," she says, "this night I'll waste in sorrow,
    "For my sick heart commands mine eyes to watch.
"Tell me, love's master, shall we meet to-morrow?
    "Say, shall we? shall we? wilt thou make the
           match?"
        He tells her, no; to-morrow he intends
        To hunt the boar with certain of his friends.

"The boar!" quoth she; whereat a sudden pale,
    Like lawn being spread upon the blushing rose,

Usurps her cheeks; she trembles at his tale,
   And on his neck her yoking arms she throws:
      She sinketh down, still hanging by his neck,
      He on her belly falls, she on her back.

Now is she in the very lists of love,
   Her champion mounted for the hot encounter:
All is imaginary she doth prove,
      He will not manage her, although he mount her,
      That worse than Tantalus' is her annoy,
      To clip Elysium, and to lack her joy.

Even as poor birds, deceiv'd with painted grapes,
   Do surfeit by the eye, and pine the maw,
Even so she languisheth in her mishaps,
      As those poor birds that helpless berries saw:
      The warm effects which she in him finds missing,
      She seeks to kindle with continual kissing.

But all in vain; good queen, it will not be:
   She hath assay'd as much as may be prov'd;
Her pleading hath deserv'd a greater fee;
      She's Love, she loves, and yet she is not lov'd.
      "Fie, fie," he says, "you crush me; let me go;
      "You have no reason to withhold me so."

"Thou hadst been gone," quoth she, "sweet boy,
      ere this,
   "But that thou told'st me, thou would'st hunt
      the boar.
"O be advis'd! thou know'st not what it is
      "With javelin's point a churlish swine to gore,
      "Whose tushes never-sheath'd he whetteth still,
      "Like to a mortal butcher, bent to kill.

"On his bow-back he hath a battle set
  "Of bristly pikes, that ever threat his foes;
"His eyes like glowworms shine when he doth fret;
  "His snout digs sepulchres where'er he goes;
    "Being mov'd, he strikes whate'er is in his way,
    "And whom he strikes, his cruel tushes slay.

"His brawny sides, with hairy bristles arm'd,
  "Are better proof than thy spear's point can enter;
"His short thick neck cannot be easily harm'd;
  "Being ireful, on the lion he will venture:
    "The thorny brambles and embracing bushes,
    "As fearful of him, part; through whom he
      rushes.

"Alas, he nought esteems that face of thine,
  "To which Love's eyes pay tributary gazes;
"Nor thy soft hands, sweet lips, and crystal eyne,
  "Whose full perfection all the world amazes;
    "But having thee at vantage (wondrous dread!)
    "Would root these beauties as he roots the mead.

"O, let him keep his loathsome cabin still!
  "Beauty hath nought to do with such foul fiends:
"Come not within his danger by thy will;
  "They that thrive well, take counsel of their friends.
    "When thou didst name the boar, not to dissemble,
    "I fear'd thy fortune, and my joints did tremble.

"Didst thou not mark my face? Was it not white?
  "Saw'st thou not signs of fear lurk in mine eye?
"Grew I not faint? And fell I not downright?
  "Within my bosom, whereon thou dost lie,
    "My boding heart pants, beats, and takes no rest,
    "But, like an earthquake, shakes thee on my
      breast.

"For where love reigns, disturbing jealousy
  "Doth call himself affection's sentinel;
"Gives false alarms, suggesteth mutiny,
    And in a peaceful hour doth cry, *kill, kill;*
      "Distempering gentle love in his desire,
      "As air and water do abate the fire.

"This sour informer, this bate-breeding spy,
  "This canker that eats up love's tender spring,
"This carry-tale, dissensious jealousy,
    "That sometime true news, sometimes false doth
        bring,
      "Knocks at my heart, and whispers in mine ear,
      "That if I love thee, I thy death should fear:

"And more than so, presenteth to mine eye
  "The picture of an angry-chafing boar,
"Under whose sharp fangs on his back doth lie
  "An image like thyself, all stain'd with gore;
    "Whose blood upon the fresh flowers being shed,
    "Doth make them droop with grief, and hang
      the head.

"What should I do, seeing thee so indeed,
  "That tremble at the imagination?
"The thought of it doth make my faint heart bleed,
  "And fear doth teach it divination:
    "I prophesy thy death, my living sorrow,
    "If thou encounter with the boar to-morrow.

"But if thou needs wilt hunt, be rul'd by me;
  Uncouple at the timorous flying hare,
"Or at the fox, which lives by subtilty,
  "Or at the roe, which no encounter dare:

"Pursue these fearful creatures o'er the downs,
"And on thy well-breath'd horse keep with thy
    hounds.

"And when thou hast on foot the purblind hare,
  "Mark the poor wretch, to overshoot his troubles,
"How he outruns the wind, and with what care
  "He cranks and crosses, with a thousand doubles:
    "The many musits through the which he goes,
    "Are like a labyrinth to amaze his foes.

"Sometime he runs among a flock of sheep,
  "To make the cunning hounds mistake their smell,
"And sometime where earth-delving conies keep,
  "To stop the loud pursuers in their yell;
    "And sometime sorteth with a herd of deer;
    "Danger deviseth shifts; wit waits on fear:

"For there his smell with others being mingled,
  "The hot scent-snuffing hounds are driven to doubt,
"Ceasing their clamorous cry till they have singled
  "With much ado the cold fault cleanly out;
    "Then do they spend their mouths: Echo
      replies,
    "As if another chase were in the skies.

"By this, poor Wat, far off upon a hill,
  "Stands on his hinder legs with listening ear,
"To hearken if his foes pursue him still;
  "Anon their loud alarums he doth hear;
    "And now his grief may be compared well
    "To one sore-sick, that hears the passing bell.

"Then shalt thou see the dew-bedabbled wretch
  "Turn, and return, indenting with the way;

"Each envious briar his weary legs doth scratch,
  "Each shadow makes him stop, each murmur stay:
    "For misery is trodden on by many,
    "And being low, never reliev'd by any.

"Lie quietly, and hear a little more;
  "Nay, do not struggle, for thou shalt not rise:
"To make thee hate the hunting of the boar,
  "Unlike myself thou hear'st me moralize,
    "Applying this to that, and so to so;
    "For love can comment upon every woe.

"Where did I leave?"—"No matter where,"
        quoth he;
  "Leave me, and then the story aptly ends:
"The night is spent." "Why, what of that?" quoth she.
  "I am," quoth he, "expected of my friends;
    "And now 'tis dark, and going I shall fall."—
    "In night," quoth she, "desire sees best of all.

"But if thou fall, O then imagine this,
  "The earth in love with thee thy footing trips,
"And all is but to rob thee of a kiss.
  "Rich preys make true men thieves; so do thy lips
    "Make modest Dian cloudy and forlorn,
    "Lest she should steal a kiss, and die forsworn.

"Now, of this dark night I perceive the reason:
  "Cynthia for shame obscures her silver shine,
"Till forging nature be condemn'd of treason,
    "For stealing moulds from heaven that were divine,
      "Wherein she fram'd thee in high heaven's
          despite
      "To shame the sun by day, and her by night.

"And therefore hath she brib'd the Destinies,
  "To cross the curious workmanship of nature,
"To mingle beauty with infirmities,
    "And pure perfection with impure defeature;
      "Making it subject to the tyranny
      "Of mad mischances and much misery;

"As burning fevers, agues pale and faint,
  "Life-poisoning pestilence, and frenzies wood,
"The marrow-eating sickness, whose attaint
    "Disorder breeds by heating of the blood:
      "Surfeits, imposthumes, grief, and damn'd
        despair,
      "Swear nature's death for framing thee so fair.

"And not the least of all these maladies,
  "But in one minute's fight brings beauty under
"Both favour, savour, hue, and qualities,
    Whereat the impartial gazer late did wonder,
      "Are on the sudden wasted, thaw'd and done,
      "As mountain-snow melts with the midday sun.

"Therefore, despite of fruitless chastity,
  "Love-lacking vestals, and self-loving nuns,
"That on the earth would breed a scarcity,
    "And barren dearth of daughters and of sons,
      "Be prodigal: the lamp that burns by night
      "Dries up his oil, to lend the world his light.

"What is thy body but a swallowing grave,
  "Seeming to bury that posterity
"Which by the rights of time thou needs must have,
    "If thou destroy them not in dark obscurity?
      "If so, the world will hold thee in disdain,
      "Sith in thy pride so fair a hope is slain.

30

"So in thyself thyself art made away;
　"A mischief worse than civil home-bred strife,
"Or theirs, whose desperate hands themselves do slay,
　"Or butcher-sire, that reaves his son of life.
　　"Foul cankering rust the hidden treasure frets,
　　"But gold that's put to use, more gold begets."

"Nay, then," quoth Adon, "you will fall again
　"Into your idle over-handled theme;
"The kiss I gave you is bestow'd in vain,
　"And all in vain you strive against the stream;
　　"For by this black-fac'd night, desire's foul nurse,
　　"Your treatise makes me like you worse and
　　　worse.

"If love have lent you twenty thousand tongues
　"And every tongue more moving than your own,
"Bewitching like the wanton mermaid's songs,
　"Yet from mine ear the tempting tune is blown;
　　"For know, my heart stands armed in mine ear
　　"And will not let a false sound enter there;

"Lest the deceiving harmony should run
　"Into the quiet closure of my breast;
"And then my little heart were quite undone,
　"In his bedchamber to be barr'd of rest.
　　"No lady, no; my heart longs not to groan,
　　"But soundly sleeps, while now it sleeps alone.

"What have you urg'd that I cannot reprove?
　"The path is smooth that leadeth on to danger;
"I hate not love, but your device in love,
　"That lends embracements unto every stranger.
　　"You do it for increase; O strange excuse!
　　"When reason is the bawd to lust's abuse.

31

"Call it not love, for love to heaven is fled,
  "Since sweating lust on earth usurp'd his name;
"Under whose simple semblance he hath fed
  "Upon fresh beauty, blotting it with blame;
    "Which the hot tyrant stains, and soon bereaves,
    "As caterpillars do the tender leaves.

"Love comforteth, like sunshine after rain,
  "But lust's effect is tempest after sun;
"Love's gentle spring doth always fresh remain,
  "Lust's winter comes ere summer half be done.
    "Love surfeits not; lust like a glutton dies:
    "Love is all truth; lust full of forged lies.

"More I could tell, but more I dare not say;
  "The text is old, the orator too green.
"Therefore, in sadness, now I will away;
  "My face is full of shame, my heart of teen;
    "Mine ears that to your wanton talk attended,
    "Do burn themselves for having so offended."

With this, he breaketh from the sweet embrace
  Of those fair arms which bound him to her breast,
And homeward through the dark lawnd runs apace;
  Leaves Love upon her back deeply distress'd.
    Look how a bright star shooteth from the sky,
    So glides he in the night from Venus' eye;

Which after him she darts, as one on shore
  Gazing upon a late-embarked friend,
Till the wild waves will have him seen no more,
  Whose ridges with the meeting clouds contend;
    So did the merciless and pitchy night
    Fold in the object that did feed her sight.

32

Whereat amaz'd, as one that unaware
   Hath dropp'd a precious jewel in the flood,
Or 'stonish'd as night-wanderers often are,
   Their light blown out in some mistrustful wood;
      Even so confounded in the dark she lay,
      Having lost the fair discovery of her way.

And now she beats her heart, whereat it groans,
   That all the neighbour-caves, as seeming troubled,
Make verbal repetition of her moans;
   Passion on passion deeply is redoubled:
      Ah me! she cries, and twenty times, *woe, woe!*
      And twenty echoes twenty times cry so.

She marking them, begins a wailing note,
   And sings extemp'rally a woful ditty;
How love makes young men thrall, and old men dote;
   How love is wise in folly, foolish-witty:
      Her heavy anthem still concludes in woe,
      And still the choir of echoes answers so.

Her song was tedious, and outwore the night,
   For lovers' hours are long, though seeming short:
If pleas'd themselves, others, they think, delight
   In such like circumstance, with such like sport:
      Their copious stories, oftentimes begun,
      End without audience, and are never done.

For who hath she to spend the night withal,
   But idle sounds, resembling parasites,
Like shrill-tongu'd tapsters answering every call,
   Soothing the humour of fantastick wits?
      She says, *'tis so*: they answer all, *'tis so;*
      And would say after her, if she said *no*.

Lo! here the gentle lark, weary of rest,
From his moist cabinet mounts up on high,
And wakes the morning, from whose silver breast
The sun ariseth in his majesty;
Who doth the world so gloriously behold,
That cedar-tops and hills seem burnish'd gold.

Venus salutes him with this fair good-morrow:
"O thou clear god, and patron of all light,
"From whom each lamp and shining star doth borrow
"The beauteous influence that makes him bright,
"There lives a son, that suck'd an earthly mother,
"May lend thee light, as thou does lend to other."

This said, she hasteth to a myrtle grove,
Musing the morning is so much o'erworn,
And yet she hears no tidings of her love:
She hearkens for his hounds, and for his horn:
Anon she hears them chaunt it lustily,
And all in haste she coasteth to the cry.

And as she runs, the bushes in the way
Some catch her by the neck, some kiss her face,
Some twine about her thigh to make her stay;
She wildly breaketh from their strict embrace,
Like a milch doe, whose swelling dugs do ache,
Hasting to feed her fawn, hid in some brake.

By this, she hears the hounds are at a bay,
Whereat she starts, like one that spies an adder
Wreath'd up in fatal folds, just in his way,
The fear whereof doth make him shake and
shudder;
Even so the timorous yelping of the hounds
Appals her senses, and her spright confounds.

For now she knows it is no gentle chase,
　　But the blunt boar, rough bear, or lion proud,
Because the cry remaineth in one place,
　　Where fearfully the dogs exclaim aloud:
　　　　Finding their enemy to be so curst,
　　　　They all strain court'sy who shall cope him first.

This dismal cry rings sadly in her ear,
　　Through which it enters to surprise her heart,
Who, overcome by doubt and bloodless fear,
　　With cold-pale weakness numbs each feeling part:
　　　　Like soldiers, when their captain once doth yield,
　　　　They basely fly, and dare not stay the field.

Thus stands she in a trembling ecstasy;
　　Till, cheering up her senses sore-dismay'd
She tells them, 'tis a causeless fantasy,
　　And childish error that they are afraid;
　　　　Bids them leave quaking, bids them fear no
　　　　　　more;—
　　　　And with that word she spied the hunted boar;

Whose frothy mouth, bepainted with all red,
　　Like milk and blood being mingled both together
A second fear through all her sinews spread,
　　Which madly hurries her she knows not whither;
　　　　This way she runs, and now she will no further,
　　　　But back retires, to rate the boar for murther.

A thousand spleens bear her a thousand ways;
　　She treads the path that she untreads again;
Her more than haste is mated with delays,
　　Like the proceedings of a drunken brain;
　　　　Full of respect, yet nought at all respecting,
　　　　In hand with all things, nought at all effecting.

Here kennel'd in a brake she finds a hound,
  And asks the weary caitiff for his master;
And there another licking of his wound,
    'Gainst venom'd sores the only sovereign plaster;
      And here she meets another sadly scowling,
      To whom she speaks; and he replies with
        howling.

When he hath ceas'd his ill-resounding noise,
  Another flap-mouth'd mourner, black and grim,
Against the welkin vollies out his voice;
    Another and another answer him,
      Clapping their proud tails to the ground below,
      Shaking their scratch'd ears, bleeding as they go.

Look, how the world's poor people are amaz'd
  At apparitions, signs, and prodigies,
Whereon with fearful eyes they long have gaz'd,
    Infusing them with dreadful prophecies:
      So she at these sad signs draws up her breath,
      And, sighing it again, exclaims on death.

"Hard-favour'd tyrant, ugly, meagre, lean,
  "Hateful divorce of love," (thus chides she death,)
"Grim-grinning ghost, earth's worm, what, dost
        thou mean
    "To stifle beauty, and to steal his breath,
      "Who when he liv'd, his breath and beauty set
      "Gloss on the rose, smell to the violet?

"If he be dead,—O no, it cannot be,
  "Seeing his beauty, thou should'st strike at it—
"O yes, it may; thou hast no eyes to see,
    "But hatefully at random dost thou hit.
      "Thy mark is feeble age; but thy false dart
      "Mistakes that aim, and cleaves an infant's heart.

"Hadst thou but bid beware, then he had spoke,
  "And hearing him, thy power had lost his power.
"The destinies will curse thee for this stroke;
  "They bid thee crop a weed, thou pluck'st a flower:
    "Love's golden arrow at him should have fled,
    "And not death's ebon dart, to strike him dead.

"Dost thou drink tears, that thou provok'st such
      weeping?
  "What may a heavy groan advantage thee?
"Why hast thou cast into eternal sleeping
  "Those eyes that taught all other eyes to see?
    "Now Nature cares not for thy mortal vigour
    "Since her best work is ruin'd with thy rigour."

Here overcome, as one full of despair,
  She vail'd her eyelids, who, like sluices, stopp'd
The crystal tide that from her two cheeks fair
  In the sweet channel of her bosom dropp'd;
    But through the flood-gates breaks the silver rain,
    And with his strong course opens them again.

O how her eyes and tears did lend and borrow!
  Her eyes seen in the tears, tears in her eye;
Both crystals, where they view'd each other's sorrow,
  Sorrow, that friendly sighs sought still to dry;
    But like a stormy day, now wind, now rain,
    Sighs dry her cheeks, tears make them wet again.

Variable passions throng her constant woe,
  As striving who should best become her grief;
All entertain'd, each passion labours so,
  That every present sorrow seemeth chief,
    But none is best; then join they all together,
    Like many clouds consulting for foul weather.

By this, far off she hears some huntsman holla;
  A nurse's song ne'er pleas'd her babe so well:
The dire imagination she did follow
    This sound of hope doth labour to expell;
      For now reviving joy bids her rejoice,
      And flatters her, it is Adonis' voice.

Whereat her tears began to turn their tide,
  Being prison'd in her eye, like pearls in glass;
Yet sometimes falls an orient drop beside,
    Which her cheek melts, as scorning it should pass,
      To wash the foul face of the sluttish ground,
      Who is but drunken when she seemeth drown'd.

O hard-believing love, how strange it seems
  Not to believe, and yet too credulous!
Thy weal and woe are both of them extremes,
    Despair and hope make thee ridiculous:
      The one doth flatter thee in thoughts unlikely,
      In likely thoughts the other kills thee quickly.

Now she unweaves the web that she hath wrought;
  Adonis lives, and death is not to blame;
It was not she that call'd him all-to naught;
    Now she adds honours to his hateful name;
      She clepes him king of graves, and grave for
        kings,
      Imperious supreme of all mortal things.

"No, no," quoth she, "sweet Death, I did but jest;
  "Yet pardon me, I felt a kind of fear,
"Whenas I met the boar, that bloody beast,
    "Which knows no pity, but is still severe;
      "Then, gentle shadow, (truth I must confess)
      "I rail'd on thee, fearing my love's decease.

" 'Tis not my fault: the boar provok'd my tongue;
  "Be wreak'd on him, invisible commander;
" 'Tis he, foul creature, that hath done thee wrong;
  "I did but act, he's author of thy slander:
    "Grief hath two tongues, and never woman yet
    "Could rule them both, without ten women's wit."

Thus, hoping that Adonis is alive,
  Her rash suspect she doth extenuate;
And that his beauty may the better thrive,
  With death she humbly doth insinuate;
    Tells him of trophies, statues, tombs; and stories
    His victories, his triumphs, and his glories.

"O Jove," quoth she, "how much a fool was I,
  "To be of such a weak and silly mind,
"To wail his death, who lives, and must not die,
  "Till mutual overthrow of mortal kind!
    "For he being dead, with him is beauty slain,
    "And, beauty dead, black chaos comes again.

"Fie, fie, fond love, thou are so full of fear
  "As one with treasure laden, hemm'd with thieves;
"Trifles, unwitnessed with eye or ear,
  "Thy coward heart with false bethinking grieves."
    Even at this word she hears a merry horn,
    Whereat she leaps, that was but late forlorn.

As falcon to the lure, away she flies;
  The grass stoops not, she treads on it so light;
And in her haste unfortunately spies
  The foul boar's conquest on her fair delight;
    Which seen, her eyes, as murder'd with the
      view,
    Like stars asham'd of day, themselves withdrew.

40

Or, as the snail, whose tender horns being hit,
  Shrinks backward in his shelly cave with pain,
And there, all smother'd up, in shade doth sit,
    Long after fearing to creep forth again;
      So, at his bloody view, her eyes are fled
      Into the deep dark cabins of her head;

Where they resign their office and their light
  To the disposing of her troubled brain;
Who bids them still consort with ugly night,
    And never wound the heart with looks again;
      Who, like a king perplexed in his throne,
      By their suggestion gives a deadly groan,

Whereat each tributary subject quakes;
  As when the wind, imprison'd in the ground,
Struggling for passage, earth's foundation shakes
    Which with cold terror doth men's minds confound:
      This mutiny each part doth so surprise,
      That from their dark beds, once more, leap
        her eyes;

And, being open'd, threw unwilling light
  Upon the wide wound that the boar had trench'd
In his soft flank; whose wonted lily white
    With purple tears, that his wound wept, was
        drench'd:
      No flower was nigh, no grass, herb, leaf, or weed,
      But stole his blood, and seem'd with him to bleed.

This solemn sympathy poor Venus noteth;
  Over one shoulder doth she hang her head;
Dumbly she passions, frantickly she doteth;
    She thinks he could not die, he is not dead.
      Her voice is stopp'd, her joints forget to bow;
      Her eyes are mad that they have wept till now.

41

Upon his hurt she looks so steadfastly,
  That her sight dazzling makes the wound seem
      three;
And then she reprehends her mangling eye,
  That makes more gashes where no breach should be:
    His face seems twain, each several limb is
      doubled;
    For oft the eye mistakes, the brain being
      troubled.

"My tongue cannot express my grief for one,
  "And yet," quoth she, "behold two Adons dead!
"My sighs are blown away, my salt tears gone,
  "Mine eyes are turn'd to fire, my heart to lead:
    "Heavy heart's lead, melt at mine eyes' red fire!
    "So shall I die by drops of hot desire.

"Alas, poor world, what treasure hast thou lost!
  "What face remains alive that's worth the viewing?
"Whose tongue is musick now? what canst thou boast
  "Of things long since, or any thing ensuing?
    "The flowers are sweet, their colours fresh and
      trim;
    "But true-sweet beauty liv'd and died with him.

"Bonnet nor veil henceforth no creature wear!
  "Nor sun nor wind will ever strive to kiss you:
"Having no fair to lose, you need not fear;
  "The sun doth scorn you, and the wind doth hiss you:
    "But when Adonis liv'd, sun and sharp air
    "Lurk'd like two thieves, to rob him of his fair;

"And therefore would he put his bonnet on,
  "Under whose brim the gaudy sun would peep;
"The wind would blow it off, and, being gone,
  "Play with his locks; then would Adonis weep:

"And straight, in pity of his tender years,
"They both would strive who first should dry
        his tears.

"To see his face, the lion walk'd along
    Behind some hedge, because he would not fear him:
"To recreate himself, when he hath sung,
    "The tiger would be tame, and gently hear him:
        "If he had spoke, the wolf would leave his prey,
        "And never fright the silly lamb that day.

"When he beheld his shadow in the brook,
    "The fishes spread on it their golden gills;
"When he was by, the birds such pleasure took,
    "That some would sing, some other in their bills
        "Would bring him mulberries, and ripe-red
            cherries;
        "He fed them with his sight, they him with
            berries.

"But this foul, grim, and urchin-snouted boar,
    "Whose downward eye still looketh for a grave,
"Ne'er saw the beauteous livery that he wore:
    "Witness the entertainment that he gave;
        "If he did see his face, why then I know,
        "He thought to kiss him, and hath kill'd him so.

" 'Tis true, 'tis true; thus was Adonis slain;
    "He ran upon the boar with his sharp spear,
"Who did not whet his teeth at him again,
    "But by a kiss thought to persuade him there;
        "And nuzzling in his flank, the loving swine
        "Sheath'd, unaware, the tusk in his soft groin.

"Had I been tooth'd like him I must confess
    "With kissing him I should have kill'd him first;

43

"But he is dead, and never did he bless
  "My youth with his; the more am I accurst."
    With this she falleth in the place she stood,
    And stains her face with his congealed blood.

She looks upon his lips, and they are pale;
  She takes him by the hand, and that is cold;
She whispers in his ears a heavy tale,
  As if they heard the woful words she told:
    She lifts the coffer-lids that close his eyes,
    Where, lo! two lamps, burnt out, in darkness lies:

Two glasses where herself herself beheld
  A thousand times, and now no more reflect;
Their virtue lost, wherein they late excell'd,
  And every beauty robb'd of his effect:
    "Wonder of time," quoth she, "this is my spite,
    "That, you being dead, the day should yet be
      light.

"Since thou art dead, lo! here I prophesy,
  "Sorrow on love hereafter shall attend;
"It shall be waited on with jealousy,
  "Find sweet beginning, but unsavoury end;
    "Ne'er settled equally, but high or low;
    "That all love's pleasure shall not match his woe.

"It shall be fickle, false, and full of fraud;
  "Bud and be blasted in a breathing while;
"The bottom poison, and the top o'erstraw'd
  "With sweets, that shall the truest sight beguile:
    "The strongest body shall it make most weak,
    "Strike the wise dumb, and teach the fool to
      speak.

"It shall be sparing, and too full of riot,
  "Teaching decrepit age to tread the measures;
"The staring ruffian shall it keep in quiet,
  "Pluck down the rich, enrich the poor with
      treasures:
    "It shall be raging mad, and silly mild,
    "Make the young old, the old become a child.

"It shall suspect where is no cause of fear;
  "It shall not fear where it should most mistrust;
"It shall be merciful, and too severe,
  "And most deceiving, when it seems most just;
    "Perverse it shall be, where it shows most
      toward,
    "Put fear to valour, courage to the coward.

"It shall be cause of war, and dire events,
  "And set dissension 'twixt the son and sire;
"Subject and servile to all discontents,
  "As dry combustious matter is to fire;
    "Sith in his prime death doth my love destroy,
    "They that love best, their loves shall not enjoy."

By this, the boy that by her side lay kill'd,
  Was melted like a vapour from her sight,
And in his blood that on the ground lay spill'd,
  A purple flower sprung up, chequer'd with white,
    Resembling well his pale cheeks, and the blood,
    Which in round drops upon their whiteness
      stood.

She bows her head, the new sprung flower to smell,
  Comparing it to her Adonis' breath;
And says, within her bosom it shall dwell,
  Since he himself is reft from her by death:

She crops the stalk, and in the breach appears
Green dropping sap, which she compares to
tears.

"Poor flower," quoth she, "this was thy father's guise,
  "(Sweet issue of a more sweet smelling sire)
"For every little grief to wet his eyes:
  "To grow unto himself was his desire,
    "And so 'tis thine; but know, it is as good
    "To wither in my breast, as in his blood.

"Here was thy father's bed, here in my breast;
  "Thou art the next of blood, and 'tis thy right:
"Lo! in this hollow cradle take thy rest,
  "My throbbing heart shall rock thee day and night:
    "There shall not be one minute in an hour
    "Wherein I will not kiss my sweet love's flower."

Thus weary of the world, away she hies,
  And yokes her silver doves; by whose swift aid
Their mistress mounted, through the empty skies
  In her light chariot quickly is convey'd,
    Holding their course to Paphos, where their
      queen
    Means to immure herself, and not be seen.

SONNETS

TO THE

ONLY BEGETTER OF THESE ENSUING SONNETS,

MR. W. H.

ALL HAPPINESS

AND THAT ETERNITY

PROMISED BY OUR EVER-LIVING POET,

WISHETH THE

WELL-WISHING ADVENTURER

IN SETTING FORTH,

T. T.[1]

[1] *T. T.*] *i. e. Thomas Thorpe.*

SONNETS

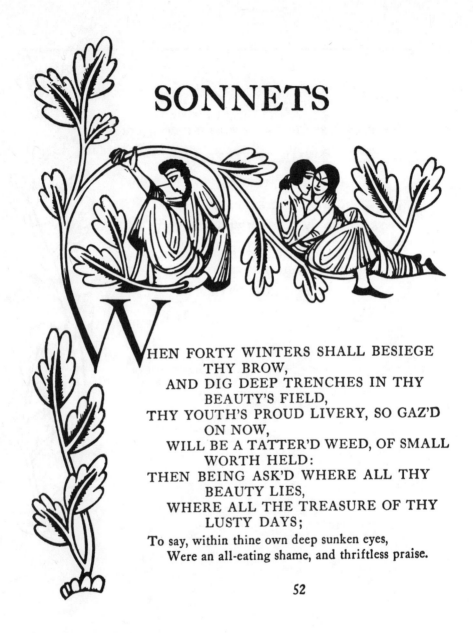

WHEN FORTY WINTERS SHALL BESIEGE
      THY BROW,
    AND DIG DEEP TRENCHES IN THY
      BEAUTY'S FIELD,
THY YOUTH'S PROUD LIVERY, SO GAZ'D
      ON NOW,
    WILL BE A TATTER'D WEED, OF SMALL
      WORTH HELD:
THEN BEING ASK'D WHERE ALL THY
      BEAUTY LIES,
    WHERE ALL THE TREASURE OF THY
      LUSTY DAYS;
To say, within thine own deep sunken eyes,
    Were an all-eating shame, and thriftless praise.

How much more praise deserv'd thy beauty's use,
    If thou could'st answer—"This fair child of mine
Shall sum my count, and make my old excuse—"
    Proving his beauty by succession thine.
        This were to be new-made when thou art old,
        And see thy blood warm when thou feel'st it
        cold.

II

From fairest creatures we desire increase,
    That thereby beauty's rose might never die,
But as the riper should by time decease,
    His tender heir might bear his memory:
But thou, contracted to thine own bright eyes,
    Feed'st thy light's flame with self-substantial fuel,
Making a famine where abundance lies,
    Thyself thy foe, to thy sweet self too cruel.
Thou that art now the world's fresh ornament,
    And only herald to the gaudy spring,
Within thine own bud buriest thy content,
    And, tender churl, mak'st waste in niggarding.
        Pity the world, or else this glutton be,
        To eat the world's due, by the grave and thee.

III

Look in thy glass, and tell the face thou viewest,
    Now is the time that face should form another;
Whose fresh repair if now thou not renewest,
    Thou dost beguile the world, unbless some mother
For where is she so fair, whose un-ear'd[1] womb
    Disdains the tillage of thy husbandry?
Or who is he so fond,[2] will be the tomb
    Of his self-love, to stop posterity?

[1] *un-ear'd*] i.e. unploughed.   [2] *fond*] i. e. foolish.

Thou art thy mother's glass, and she in thee
    Calls back the lovely April of her prime:
So thou through windows of thine age shalt see,
    Despite of wrinkles, this thy golden time.
        But if thou live, remember'd not to be,
        Die single, and thine image dies with thee.

IV

Unthrifty loveliness, why dost thou spend
    Upon thyself thy beauty's legacy?
Nature's bequest gives nothing, but doth lend,
    And being frank, she lends to those are free.
Then, beauteous niggard, why dost thou abuse
    The bounteous largess given thee to give?
Profitless usurer, why dost thou use
    So great a sum of sums, yet canst not live?
For having traffick with thyself alone,
    Thou of thyself thy sweet self dost deceive.
Then how, when nature calls thee to be gone,
    What acceptable audit canst thou leave?
        Thy unus'd beauty must be tomb'd with thee,
        Which, us'd, lives thy executor to be.

V

Those hours, that with gentle work did frame
    The lovely gaze where every eye doth dwell,
Will play the tyrants to the very same,
    And that unfair[3] which fairly doth excell;
For never-resting time leads summer on
    To hideous winter, and confounds him there;
Sap check'd with frost, and lusty leaves quite gone,
    Beauty o'ersnow'd, and bareness every where:
Then, were not summer's distillation left,
    A liquid prisoner pent in walls of glass,

3 *unfair*] i. e. deprive of beauty.

54

Beauty's effect with beauty were bereft,
    Nor it, nor no remembrance what it was.
        But flowers distill'd, though they with winter
            meet,
        Leese[4] but their show; their substance still lives
            sweet.

VI

Then let not winter's ragged hand deface
    In thee thy summer, ere thou be distill'd:
Make sweet some phial; treasure thou some place
    With beauty's treasure, ere it be self-kill'd.
That use[5] is not forbidden usury,
    Which happies those that pay the willing loan;
That's for thyself to breed another thee,
    Or ten times happier, be it ten for one;
Ten times thyself were happier than thou art,
    If ten of thine ten times refigur'd thee:
Then, what could death do if thou should'st depart,
    Leaving thee living in posterity?
        Be not self-will'd, for thou art much too fair
        To be death's conquest, and make worms thine
           heir.

VII

Lo, in the orient when the gracious light
    Lifts up his burning head, each under eye
Doth homage to his new-appearing sight,
    Serving with looks his sacred majesty;
And having climb'd the steep-up heavenly hill,
    Resembling strong youth in his middle age,
Yet mortal looks adore his beauty still,
    Attending on his golden pilgrimage;

4 *leese*] i. e. lose.   5 *use*] i. e. usance.

But when from high-most pitch, with weary car,
   Like feeble age, he reeleth from the day,
The eyes, 'fore duteous, now converted are
   From his low tract, and look another way:
     So thou, thyself outgoing in thy noon,
     Unlook'd on diest, unless thou get a son.

VIII

Musick to hear, why hear'st thou musick sadly;
   Sweets with sweets war not, joy delights in joy.
Why lov'st thou that which thou receiv'st not gladly?
   Or else receiv'st with pleasure thine annoy?
If the true concord of well-tuned sounds,
   By unions married, do offend thine ear,
They do but sweetly chide thee, who confounds
   In singleness the parts that thou should'st bear.
Mark how one string, sweet husband to another,
   Strikes each in each by mutual ordering;
Resembling sire and child and happy mother,
   Who all in one, one pleasing note do sing:
     Whose speechless song, being many, seeming
      one,
     Sings this to thee, "thou single wilt prove none."

IX

Is it for fear to wet a widow's eye,
   That thou consum'st thyself in single life?
Ah, if thou issueless shalt hap to die,
   The world will wail thee, like a makeless[7] wife:
The world will be thy widow, and still weep,
   That thou no form of thee hast left behind,
When every private widow well may keep,
   By children's eyes, her husband's shape in mind.

[7] *makeless*] i. e. mateless

Look, what an unthrift in the world doth spend,
 Shifts but his place, for still the world enjoys it;
But beauty's waste hath in the world an end,
 And kept unus'd, the user so destroys it.
  No love toward others in that bosom sits,
  That on himself such murderous shame
   commits.

X

For shame! deny that thou bear'st love to any,
 Who for thyself art so unprovident.
Grant if thou wilt, thou art belov'd of many,
 But that thou none lov'st, is most evident;
For thou art so possess'd with murderous hate,
 That 'gainst thyself thou stick'st not to conspire,
Seeking that beauteous roof to ruinate,
 Which to repair should be thy chief desire.
O change thy thought, that I may change my mind!
 Shall hate be fairer lodg'd than gentle love?
Be, as thy presence is, gracious and kind,
 Or to thyself, at least, kind-hearted prove;
  Make thee another self, for love of me,
  That beauty still may live in thine or thee.

XI

As fast as thou shalt wane, so fast thou grow'st
 In one of thine, from that which thou departest;
And that fresh blood which youngly thou bestow'st,
 Thou may'st call thine, when thou from youth
  convertest.
Herein lives wisdom, beauty, and increase;
 Without this, folly, age, and cold decay:
If all were minded so, the times should cease,
 And threescore years would make the world away.

Let those whom nature hath not made for store,[8]
    Harsh, featureless, and rude, barrenly perish:
Look whom she best endow'd, she gave thee more;
    Which bounteous gift thou should'st in bounty
            cherish;
        She carv'd thee for her seal, and meant thereby,
        Thou should'st print more, nor let that copy die.

XII

When I do count the clock that tells the time,
    And see the brave day sunk in hideous night;
When I behold the violet past prime,
    And sable curls, all silver'd o'er with white;
When lofty trees I see barren of leaves,
    Which erst from heat did canopy the herd,
And summer's green all girded up in sheaves,
    Borne on the bier with white and bristly beard;
Then of thy beauty do I question make,
    That thou among the wastes of time must go,
Since sweets and beauties do themselves forsake,
    And die as fast as they see others grow;
        And nothing 'gainst time's scythe can make
            defence,
        Save breed, to brave him when he takes thee
            hence.

XIII

O that you were yourself! but, love, you are
    No longer yours, than you yourself here live:
Against this coming end you should prepare,
    And your sweet semblance to some other give.
So should that beauty which you hold in lease
    Find no determination: then you were

8 *for store*] "i. e. to be preserved for use." MALONE.

Yourself again, after yourself's decease,
    When your sweet issue your sweet form should bear.
Who lets so fair a house fall to decay,
    Which husbandry in honour might uphold
Against the stormy gusts of winter's day,
    And barren rage of death's eternal cold?
        O! none but unthrifts:—Dear my love, you
            know
        You had a father; let your son say so.

XIV

Not from the stars do I my judgment pluck;
    And yet methinks I have astronomy,
But not to tell of good, or evil luck,
    Of plagues, of dearths, or season's quality:
Nor can I fortune to brief minutes tell,
    Pointing to each his thunder, rain, and wind,
Or say, with princes if it shall go well,
    By oft predict that I in heaven find:
But from thine eyes my knowledge I derive,
    And (constant stars) in them I read such art,
As truth and beauty shall together thrive,
    If from thyself to store thou would'st convert:[9]
        Or else of thee this I prognosticate,
        Thy end is truth's and beauty's doom and date.

XV

When I consider every thing that grows
    Holds in perfection but a little moment,
That this huge state presenteth nought but shows
    Whereon the stars in secret influence comment;
When I perceive that men as plants increase,
    Cheered and check'd even by the selfsame sky;

    [9] *If from thyself to store thou would'st convert*] "i. e. if thou wouldest change thy single state, and beget a numerous progeny." MALONE.

Vaunt in their youthful sap, at height decrease,
And wear their brave state out of memory;
Then the conceit of this inconstant stay
Sets you most rich in youth before my sight,
Where wasteful time debateth with decay,
To change your day of youth to sullied night;
And, all in war with time, for love of you,
As he takes from you, I engraft you new.

XVI

But wherefore do not you a mightier way
Make war upon this bloody tyrant, Time?
And fortify yourself in your decay
With means more blessed than my barren rhyme?
Now stand you on the top of happy hours;
And many maiden gardens, yet unset,
With virtuous wish would bear you living flowers,
Much liker than your painted counterfeit:[10]
So should the lines of life that life repair,
Which this, Time's pencil, or my pupil pen,
Neither in inward worth, nor outward fair,[11]
Can make you live yourself in eyes of men.
To give away yourself, keeps yourself still;
And you must live, drawn by your own sweet
skill.

XVII

Who will believe my verse in time to come,
If it were fill'd with your most high deserts?
Though yet heaven knows, it is but as a tomb
Which hides your life, and shows not half your
parts.

10 *counterfeit*] i. e. portrait.
11 *fair*] i. e. beauty.

60

If I could write the beauty of your eyes,
    And in fresh numbers number all your graces,
The age to come would say, this poet lies,
    Such heavenly touches ne'er touch'd earthly faces.
So should my papers, yellow'd with their age,
    Be scorn'd, like old men of less truth than tongue;
And your true rights be term'd a poet's rage,
    And stretched metre of an antique song:
        But were some child of yours alive that time,
        You should live twice;—in it, and in my rhyme.

XVIII

Shall I compare thee to a summer's day?
    Thou art more lovely and more temperate:
Rough winds do shake the darling buds of May,
    And summer's lease hath all too short a date:
Sometime too hot the eye of heaven shines,
    And often is his gold complexion dimm'd;
And every fair from fair sometime declines,
    By chance, or nature's changing course, untrimm'd;
But thy eternal summer shall not fade,
    Nor lose possession of that fair[12] thou owest;
Nor shall death brag thou wander'st in his shade,
    When in eternal lines to time thou growest;
        So long as men can breathe, or eyes can see,
        So long lives this, and this gives life to thee.

XIX

Devouring Time, blunt thou the lion's paws,
    And make the earth devour her own sweet brood;
Pluck the keen teeth from the fierce tiger's jaws,
    And burn the long-liv'd phoenix in her blood;

    12 *fair*] i. e. beauty.

Make glad and sorry seasons, as thou fleets,[13]
    And do whate'er thou wilt, swift-footed Time,
To the wide world, and all her fading sweets;
    But I forbid thee one most heinous crime:
O carve not with thy hours my love's fair brow,
    Nor draw no lines there with thine antique pen;
Him in thy course untainted do allow,
    For beauty's pattern to succeeding men.
        Yet, do thy worst, old Time: despite thy wrong,
        My love shall in my verse ever live young.

XX

A woman's face, with nature's own hand painted,
    Hast thou, the master-mistress of my passion;
A woman's gentle heart, but not acquainted
    With shifting change, as is false women's fashion;
An eye more bright than theirs, less false in rolling,
    Gilding the object whereupon it gazeth;
A man in hue, all hue in his controlling,
    Which steals men's eyes, and women's souls
        amazeth.
And for a woman wert thou first created;
    Till nature, as she wrought thee, fell a-doting,
And by addition me of thee defeated,
    By adding one thing to my purpose nothing.
        But since she prick'd[14] thee out for women's
        pleasure,
        Mine be thy love, and thy love's use their
        treasure.

13 *fleets*] i. e. *fleetest*,—for the sake of the rhyme.

14 *prick'd*] i. e. marked.

XXI

So is it not with me as with that muse,
   Stirr'd by a painted beauty to his verse;
Who heaven itself for ornament doth use,
   And every fair with his fair doth rehearse;
Making a couplement of proud compare,
   With sun and moon, with earth and sea's rich gems,
With April's first-born flowers, and all things rare
   That heaven's air in his huge rondure[15] hems.
O let me, true in love, but truly write,
   And then believe me, my love is as fair
As any mother's child, though not so bright
   As those gold candles fix'd in heaven's air:
      Let them say more that like of hear-say well;
      I will not praise, that purpose not to sell.

XXII

My glass shall not persuade me I am old,
   So long as youth and thou are of one date;
But when in thee time's furrows I behold,
   Then look I death my days should expiate.[16]
For all that beauty doth cover thee,
   Is but the seemly raiment of my heart,
Which in thy breast doth live, as thine in me;
   How can I then be elder than thou art?
O therefore, love, be of thyself so wary,
   As I not for myself but for thee will;
Bearing thy heart, which I will keep so chary
   As tender nurse her babe from faring ill.
      Presume not on thy heart when mine is slain;
      Thou gav'st me thine, not to give back again.

[15] *rondure*] i. e. round, circumference.

[16] *expiate*] "i. e. fill up the measure of." MALONE.

XXIII

As an unperfect actor on the stage,
  Who with his fear is put beside his part,
Or some fierce thing replete with too much rage,
  Whose strength's abundance weakens his own heart;
So I, for fear of trust, forget to say
  The perfect ceremony of love's rite,
And in mine own love's strength seem to decay,
  O'ercharg'd with burthen of mine own love's might.
O let my books be then the eloquence
  And dumb presagers of my speaking breast;
Who plead for love, and look for recompense,
  More than that tongue that more hath more
      express'd.
      O learn to read what silent love hath writ:
      To hear with eyes belongs to love's fine wit.

XXIV

Mine eyes hath play'd the painter, and hath stell'd[17]
  Thy beauty's form in table of my heart;
My body is the frame wherein 'tis held,
  And perspective it is best painter's art.
For through the painter must you see his skill,
  To find where your true image pictur'd lies,
Which in my bosom's shop is hanging still,
  That hath his windows glazed with thine eyes.
Now see what good turns eyes for eyes have done;
  Mine eyes have drawn thy shape, and thine for me
Are windows to my breast, where-through the sun
  Delights to peep, to gaze therein on thee;
      Yet eyes this cunning want to grace their art,
      They draw but what they see, know not the
          heart.

17 *stell'd*] i. e. fixed.

64

XXV

Let those who are in favour with their stars,
    Of publick honour and proud titles boast,
Whilst I, whom fortune of such triumph bars,
    Unlook'd for joys in that I honour most.
Great princes' favourites their fair leaves spread,
    But as the marigold at the sun's eye;
And in themselves their pride lies buried,
    For at a frown they in their glory die.
The painful warrior famoused for fight,
    After a thousand victories once foil'd,
Is from the book of honour razed quite,
    And all the rest forgot for which he toil'd:
        Then happy I, that love and am belov'd,
        Where I may not remove, nor be remov'd.

XXVI

Lord of my love, to whom in vassalage
    Thy merit hath my duty strongly knit,
To thee I send this written embassage,
    To witness duty, not to show my wit.
Duty so great, which wit so poor as mine
    May make seem bare, in wanting words to show it;
But that I hope some good conceit of thine
    In thy soul's thought, all naked, will bestow it:
Till whatsoever star that guides by moving,
    Points on me graciously with fair aspéct,
And puts apparel on my tatter'd loving
    To show me worthy of thy sweet respect:
        Then may I dare to boast how I do love thee,
        Till then, not show my head where thou may'st
           prove me.

XXVII

Weary with toil, I haste me to my bed,
    The dear repose for limbs with travel tir'd;
But then begins a journey in my head,
    To work my mind, when body's work's expir'd:
For then my thoughts (from far where I abide)
    Intend a zealous pilgrimage to thee,
And keep my drooping eyelids open wide,
    Looking on darkness which the blind do see:

Save that my soul's imaginary sight
  Presents thy shadow to my sightless view,
Which, like a jewel hung in ghastly night,
    Makes black night beauteous, and her old face new.
      Lo, thus, by day my limbs, by night my mind,
      For thee, and for myself, no quiet find.

XXVIII

How can I then return in happy plight,
  That am debarr'd the benefit of rest?
When day's oppression is not eas'd by night,
  But day by night and night by day oppress'd?
And each, though enemies to either's reign,
  Do in consent shake hands to torture me,
The one by toil, the other to complain
  How far I toil, still farther off from thee.
I tell the day, to please him, thou art bright,
  And dost him grace when clouds do blot the
      heaven:
So flatter I the swart-complexion'd night;
  When sparkling stars twire[19] not, thou gild'st the
      even.
    But day both daily draw my sorrows longer,
    And night doth nightly make grief's length
      seem stronger.

XXIX

When in disgrace with fortune and men's eyes,
  I all alone beweep my outcast state,
And trouble deaf heaven with my bootless cries,
  And look upon myself, and curse my fate,
Wishing me like to one more rich in hope,
  Featur'd like him, like him with friends possess'd,

19 *twire*] i. e. peep out.

Desiring this man's art, and that man's scope,
　With what I most enjoy contented least;
Yet in these thoughts myself almost despising,
　Haply I think on thee,—and then my state
(Like to the lark at break of day arising
　　From sullen earth) sings hymns at heaven's gate;
　　For thy sweet love remember'd, such wealth
　　　brings,
　　That then I scorn to change my state with kings.

XXX

When to the sessions of sweet silent thought
　I summon up remembrance of things past,
I sigh the lack of many a thing I sought,
　And with old woes new wail my dear times' waste:
Then can I drown an eye, unus'd to flow,
　For precious friends hid in death's dateless night,
And weep afresh love's long-since cancell'd woe,
　And moan the expense of many a vanish'd sight.
Then can I grieve at grievances fore-gone,
　And heavily from woe to woe tell o'er
The sad account of fore-bemoaned moan,
　Which I new pay as if not paid before.
　　But if the while I think on thee, dear friend,
　　All losses are restor'd, and sorrows end.

XXXI

Thy bosom is endeared with all hearts,
　Which I by lacking have supposed dead;
And there reigns love and all love's loving parts,
　And all those friends which I thought buried.
How many a holy and obsequious[20] tear
　Hath dear religious love stolen from mine eye,

20 *obsequious*] i. e. funereal.

68

As interest of the dead, which now appear
    But things remov'd, that hidden in thee lie;
Thou art the grave where buried love doth live,
    Hung with the trophies of my lovers gone,
Who all their parts of me to thee did give;
    That due of many now is thine alone:
        Their images I lov'd I view in thee,
        And thou (all they) hast all the all of me.

XXXII

If thou survive my well contented day,
    When that churl Death my bones with dust shall cover,
And shalt by fortune once more re-survey
    These poor rude lines of thy deceased lover,
Compare them with the bettering of the time;
    And though they be outstripp'd by every pen,
Reserve them for my love, not for their rhyme,
    Exceeded by the height of happier men.
O then vouchsafe me but this loving thought!
   Had my friend's muse grown with this growing age,
A dearer birth than this his love had brought,
   To march in ranks of better equipage:
     But since he died, and poets better prove,
     Theirs for their style I'll read, his for his love.

XXXIII

Full many a glorious morning have I seen
    Flatter the mountain tops with sovereign eye,
Kissing with golden face the meadows green,
    Gilding pale streams with heavenly alchymy
Anon permit the basest clouds to ride
    With ugly rack[21] on his celestial face,
And from the forlorn world his visage hide,
    Stealing unseen to west with this disgrace:

21 *rack*] i.e. vapours.

Even so my sun one early morn did shine,
    With all triumphant splendour on my brow;
But out! alack! he was but one hour mine,
    The region cloud hath mask'd him from me now.
        Yet him for this my love no whit disdaineth;
        Suns of the world may stain, when heaven's sun
        staineth.

XXXIV

Why dost thou promise such a beauteous day,
    And make me travel forth without my cloak,
To let base clouds o'ertake me in my way,
    Hiding thy bravery in their rotten smoke?
'Tis not enough that through the cloud thou break,
    To dry the rain on my storm-beaten face,
For no man well of such a salve can speak,
    That heals the wound, and cures not the disgrace:
Nor can thy shame give physic to my grief;
    Though thou repent, yet I have still the loss:
The offender's sorrow lends but weak relief
    To him that bears the strong offence's cross.
        Ah! but those tears are pearl which thy love
        sheds,
    And they are rich, and ransom all ill deeds.

XXXV

No more be griev'd at that which thou hast done:
    Roses have thorns, and silver fountains mud;
Clouds and eclipses stain both moon and sun,
    And loathsome canker lives in sweetest bud.
All men make faults, and even I in this,
    Authórising thy trespass with compare,
Myself corrupting, salving thy amiss,[22]
    Excusing thy sins more than thy sins are:

[22] *amiss*] i. e. fault.

For to thy sensual fault I bring in sense,
    (Thy adverse party is thy advocate)
And 'gainst myself a lawful plea commence:
    Such civil war is in my love and hate,
        That I an accessory needs must be
        To that sweet thief, which sourly robs from me.

XXXVI

Let me confess that we two must be twain,
    Although our undivided loves are one:
So shall those blots that do with me remain,
    Without thy help, by me be borne alone.
In our two loves there is but one respect,
    Though in our lives a separable spite,[23]
Which though it alter not love's sole effect,
    Yet doth it steal sweet hours from love's delight.
I may not evermore acknowledge thee,
    Lest my bewailed guilt should do thee shame;
Nor thou with public kindness honour me,
    Unless thou take that honour from thy name:
        But do not so; I love thee in such sort,
        As thou being mine, mine is thy good report.

XXXVII

As a decrepit father takes delight
    To see his active child do deeds of youth,
So I, made lame by fortune's dearest[24] spite,
    Take all my comfort of thy worth and truth;
For whether beauty, birth, or wealth, or wit,
    Or any of these all, or all, or more,

---

[23] *separable spite*] "i. e. a cruel fate, that spitefully separates us from each other. *Separable* for *separating*." MALONE.

[24] *dearest*] i. e. excessive, grievous.

Entitled in thy parts[25] do crowned sit,
    I make my love engrafted to this store:
So then I am not lame, poor, nor despis'd,
    Whilst that this shadow doth such substance give,
That I in thy abundance am suffic'd,
    And by a part of thy glory live.
        Look what is best, that best I wish in thee;
        This wish I have; then ten times happy me!

XXXVIII

How can my muse want subject to invent,
    While thou dost breathe, that pour'st into my verse
Thine own sweet argument, too excellent
    For every vulgar paper to rehearse?
O, give thyself the thanks, if aught in me
    Worthy perusal stand against thy sight;
For who's so dumb that cannot write to thee,
    When thou thyself dost give invention light?
Be thou the tenth muse, ten times more in worth
    Than those old nine, which rhymers invocate;
And he that calls on thee, let him bring forth
    Eternal numbers to outlive long date.
        If my slight muse do please these curious days,
        The pain be mine, but thine shall be the praise.

XXXIX

O, how thy worth with manners may I sing,
    When thou art all the better part of me?
What can mine own praise to mine own self bring?
    And what is't but mine own, when I praise thee?
Even for this let us divided live,
    And our dear love lose name of single one,
That by this separation I may give
    That due to thee, which thou deserv'st alone.

25 *entitled in thy parts*] i. e. having a claim or title to thy parts.

O absence, what a torment would'st thou prove.
  Were it not thy sour leisure gave sweet leave
To entertain the time with thoughts of love,
  (Which time and thoughts so sweetly doth
      deceive,)
    And that thou teachest how to make one twain,
    By praising him here, who doth hence remain.

XL

Take all my loves, my love, yea, take them all;
  What hast thou then more than thou hadst before?
No love, my love, that thou may'st true love call;
  All mine was thine, before thou hadst this more.
Then if for my love thou my love receivest,
  I cannot blame thee, for my love thou usest;
But yet be blam'd, if thou thyself deceivest
  By wilful taste of what thyself refusest.
I do forgive thy robbery, gentle thief,
  Although thou steal thee all my poverty;
And yet love knows, it is a greater grief
  To bear love's wrong, than hate's known injury.
    Lascivious grace, in whom all ill well shows,
    Kill me with spites; yet we must not be foes.

XLI

Those pretty wrongs that liberty commits,
  When I am sometimes absent from thy heart,
Thy beauty and thy years full well befits,
  For still temptation follows where thou art.
Gentle thou art, and therefore to be won,
  Beauteous thou art, therefore to be assail'd;
And when a woman woos, what woman's son
  Will sourly leave her till she have prevail'd.
Ah me! but yet thou might'st my seat forbear,
  And chide thy beauty and thy straying youth,

73

Who lead thee in their riot even there
  Where thou art forc'd to break a two-fold truth;
    Hers, by thy beauty tempting her to thee,
    Thine, by thy beauty being false to me.

XLII

That thou hast her, it is not all my grief,
  And yet it may be said I lov'd her dearly;
That she hath thee, is of my wailing chief,
  A loss in love that touches me more nearly.
Loving offenders, thus I will excuse ye:—
  Thou dost love her, because thou knew'st I love
      her;
And for my sake even so doth she abuse me,
  Suffering my friend for my sake to approve her.
If I lose thee, my loss is my love's gain,
  And losing her, my friend hath found that loss;
Both find each other, and I lose both twain,
  And both for my sake lay on me this cross:
    But here's the joy; my friend and I are one;
    Sweet flattery! then she loves but me alone.

XLIII

When most I wink, then do mine eyes best see,
  For all the day they view things unrespected;[26]
But when I sleep, in dreams they look on thee,
  And darkly bright, are bright iu dark directed;
Then thou whose shadow shadows doth make bright,
  How would thy shadow's form form happy show
To the clear day with thy much clearer light,
  When to unseeing eyes thy shade shines so?
How would (I say) mine eyes be blessed made
  By looking on thee in the living day,

26 unrespected] i. e. unregarded.

74

When in dead night thy fair imperfect shade
    Through heavy sleep on sightless eyes doth stay?
        All days are nights to see, till I see thee,
        And nights, bright days, when dreams do show
            thee me.

XLIV

If the dull substance of my flesh were thought,
    Injurious distance should not stop my way;
For then, despite of space, I would be brought
    From limits far remote, where thou dost stay.
No matter then, although my foot did stand
    Upon the farthest earth remov'd from thee,
For nimble thought can jump both sea and land,
    As soon as think the place where he would be.
But ah! thought kills me, that I am not thought,
    To leap large lengths of miles when thou art gone,
But that, so much of earth and water wrought,[27]
    I must attend time's leisure with my moan;
        Receiving nought by elements so slow
        But heavy tears, badges of either's woe:

XLV

The other two, slight air and purging fire,
    Are both with thee, wherever I abide;
The first my thought, the other my desire,
    These present-absent with swift motion slide.
For when these quicker elements are gone
    In tender embassy of love to thee,
My life being made of four, with two alone,
    Sinks down to death, oppress'd with melancholy;

[27] *so much of earth and water wrought*] "i. e. being so thoroughly com-
pounded of these two ponderous elements." STEEVENS.

Until life's composition be recur'd
    By those swift messengers return'd from thee,
Who even but now come back again, assur'd
    Of thy fair health, recounting it to me:
        This told, I joy; but then no longer glad,
        I send them back again, and straight grow **sad**.

XLVI

Mine eye and heart are at a mortal war,
    How to divide the conquest of thy sight;
Mine eye my heart thy picture's sight would bar,
    My heart mine eye the freedom of that right.
My heart doth plead, that thou in him dost lie,
    (A closet never pierc'd with crystal eyes,)
But the defendant doth that plea deny,
    And says in him thy fair appearance lies.
To 'cide[28] this title is impannelled
    A quest of thoughts, all tenants to the heart;
And by their verdict is determined
    The clear eye's moiety,[29] and the dear heart's part:
        As thus; mine eye's due is thine outward part
        And my heart's right thine inward love of heart.

XLVII

Betwixt mine eye and heart a league is took,
    And each doth good turns now unto the other:
When that mine eye is famish'd for a look,
    Or heart in love with sighs himself doth smother,
With my love's picture then my eye doth feast,
    And to the painted banquet bids my heart:
Another time mine eye is my heart's guest,
    And in his thoughts of love doth share a part:

28 *'cide*] i. e. decide.
29 *moiety*] i. e. portion.

76

So, either by thy picture or my love,
    Thyself away art present still with me;
For thou not farther than my thoughts canst move,
    And I am still with them, and they with thee;
        Or if they sleep, thy picture in my sight
        Awakes my heart to heart's and eye's delight.

XLVIII

How careful was I when I took my way,
    Each trifle under truest bars to thrust,
That, to my use, it might unused stay
    From hands of falsehood, in sure wards of trust!
But thou, to whom my jewels trifles are,
    Most worthy comfort, now my greatest grief,
Thou, best of dearest, and mine only care,
    Art left the prey of every vulgar thief.
Thee have I not lock'd up in any chest,
    Save where thou art not, though I feel thou art,
Within the gentle closure of my breast,
    From whence at pleasure thou may'st come and
        part;
        And even thence thou wilt be stolen I fear,
        For truth proves thievish for a prize so dear.

XLIX

Against that time, if ever that time come,
    When I shall see thee frown on my defects,
Whenas thy love hath cast his utmost sum,
    Call'd to that audit by advis'd respects;
Against that time, when thou shalt strangely pass,
    And scarcely greet me with that sun, thine eye,
When love, converted from the thing it was,
    Shall reasons find of settled gravity;

Against that time do I esconce[30] me here
    Within the knowledge of mine own desert,
And this my hand against myself uprear,
    To guard the lawful reasons on thy part:
        To leave poor me thou hast the strength of laws,
        Since, why to love, I can allege no cause.

L

How heavy do I journey on the way,
    When what I seek,—my weary travel's end,—
Doth teach that ease and that repose to say,
    "Thus far the miles are measur'd from thy friend!"
The beast that bears me, tired with my woe,
    Plods dully on, to bear that weight in me,
As if by some instinct the wretch did know
    His rider lov'd not speed, being made from thee:
The bloody spur cannot provoke him on
    That sometimes anger thrusts into his hide,
Which heavily he answers with a groan,
    More sharp to me than spurring to his side;
        For that same groan doth put this in my mind,
        My grief lies onward, and my joy behind.

LI

Thus can my love excuse the slow offence
    Of my dull bearer, when from thee I speed:
From where thou art why should I haste me thence?
    Till I return, of posting is no need.
O, what excuse will my poor beast then find,
    When swift extremity can seem but slow?
Then should I spur, though mounted on the wind;
    In winged speed no motion shall I know:
Then can no horse with my desire keep pace;

30 *ensconce*] i. e. fortify.

78

Therefore desire, of perfect love being made,
Shall neigh (no dull flesh) in his fiery race;
But love, for love, thus shall excuse my jade;
Since from thee going he went wilful slow,
Towards thee I'll run, and give him leave to go.

LII

So am I as the rich, whose blessed key
Can bring him to his sweet up-locked treasure,
The which he will not every hour survey,
For blunting the fine point of seldom pleasure.
Therefore are feasts[31] so solemn and so rare,
Since seldom coming, in the long year set,
Like stones of worth they thinly placed are,
Or captain[32] jewels in the carcanet.[33]
So is the time that keeps you, as my chest,
Or as the wardrobe which the robe doth hide,
To make some special instant special-blest,
By new unfolding his imprison'd pride.
Blessed are you, whose worthiness gives scope,
Being had, to triumph, being lack'd, to hope.

LIII

What is your substance, whereof are you made,
That millions of strange shadows on you tend?
Since every one hath, every one, one's shade,
And you, but one, can every shadow lend.
Describe Adonis, and the counterfeit[34]
Is poorly imitated after you;
On Helen's cheek all art of beauty set,
And you in Grecian tires are painted new:

[31] *feasts*] "He means the four *festivals* of the year." STEEVENS.
[32] *captain*] i. e. chief, more valuable.
[33] *carcanet*] i. e. necklace.
[34] *counterfeit*] i.e. portrait.

79

Speak of the spring, and foizon[35] of the year;
   The one doth shadow of your beauty show,
The other as your bounty doth appear,
   And you in every blessed shape we know.
      In all external grace you have some part,
      But you like none, none you, for constant heart.

LIV

O how much more doth beauty beauteous seem,
   By that sweet ornament which truth doth give!
The rose looks fair, but fairer we it deem
   For that sweet odour which doth in it live.
The canker-blooms[36] have full as deep a dye,
   As the perfumed tincture of the roses,
Hang on such thorns, and play as wantonly
   When summer's breath their masked buds discloses:
But, for their virtue only is their show,
   They live unwoo'd, and unrespected fade;
Die to themselves. Sweet roses do not so;
   Of their sweet deaths are sweetest odours made:
      And so of you, beauteous and lovely youth,
      When that shall fade, by verse distills your
      truth.

LV

Not marble, nor the gilded monuments
   Of princes, shall out-live this powerful rhyme:
But you shall shine more bright in these contents
   Than unswept stone, besmear'd with sluttish time.
When wasteful war shall statues overturn,
   And broils root out the work of masonry,
Nor Mars his sword nor war's quick fire shall burn
   The living record of your memory.

35 *foizon*] i. e. plenty.
36 *canker-blooms*] i. e. the blossoms of the *canker*,—the wild, or dog-rose.

80

'Gainst death and all-oblivious enmity
  Shall you pace forth; your praise shall still find
      room,
Even in the eyes of all posterity
  That wear this world out to the ending doom.
    So till the judgment that yourself arise,
    You live in this, and dwell in lovers' eyes.

LVI

Sweet love, renew thy force; be it not said,
  Thy edge should blunter be than appetite,
Which but to-day by feeding is allay'd,
  To-morrow sharpen'd in his former might:
So, love, be thou; although to-day thou fill
  Thy hungry eyes, even till they wink with fulness,
To-morrow see again, and do not kill
  The spirit of love with a perpetual dulness.
Let this sad interim like the ocean be
  Which parts the shore, where two contracted-new
Come daily to the banks, that, when they see
  Return of love, more blest may be the view;
    Or call it winter, which, being full of care,
    Makes summer's welcome thrice more wish'd,
        more rare.

LVII

Being your slave, what should I do but tend
  Upon the hours and times of your desire?
I have no precious time at all to spend,
  Nor services to do, till you require.
Nor dare I chide the world-without-end hour,[38]
  Whilst I, my sovereign, watch the clock for you,
Nor think the bitterness of absence sour,
  When you have bid your servant once adieu;

[38] *the world-without-end hour*] i. e. the hour that seems as if it never
would end.

Nor dare I question with my jealous thought
   Where you may be, or your affairs suppose,
But, like a sad slave, stay and think of nought,
   Save, where you are how happy you make those:
     So true a fool is love, that in your will
     (Though you do any thing) he thinks no ill.

LVIII

That God forbid, that made me first your slave,
   I should in thought control your times of pleasure,
Or at your hand the account of hours to crave,
   Being your vassal, bound to stay your leisure!
O, let me suffer (being at your beck)
   The imprison'd absence of your liberty,
And patience, tame to sufferance, bide each check
   Without accusing you of injury.
Be where you list; your charter is so strong,
   That you yourself may privilege your time:
Do what you will, to you it doth belong
   Yourself to pardon of self-doing crime.
     I am to wait, though waiting so be hell;
     Not blame you pleasure, be it ill or well.

LIX

If there be nothing new, but that, which is,
   Hath been before, how are our brains beguil'd,
Which labouring for invention bear amiss
   The second burthen of a former child?
O, that record could with a backward look,
   Even of five hundred courses of the sun,
Show me your image in some antique book,
   Since mind at first in character was done!
That I might see what the old world could say
   To this composed wonder of your frame;

Whether we are mended, or whe'r[39] better they,
   Or whether revolution be the same.
      O! sure I am, the wits of former days
      To subjects worse have given admiring praise.

LX

Like as the waves make towards the pebbled shore,
   So do our minutes hasten to their end;
Each changing place with that which goes before,
   In sequent toil all forwards do contend.
Nativity once in the main of light,[40]
   Crawls to maturity, wherewith being crown'd.
Crooked eclipses 'gainst his glory fight,
   And time that gave, doth now his gift confound.
Time doth transfix the flourish set on youth,
   And delves the parallels in beauty's brow;
Feeds on the rarities of nature's truth,
   And nothing stands but for his scythe to mow.
      And yet, to times in hope, my verse shall stand,
      Praising thy worth, despite his cruel hand.

LXI

Is it thy will, thy image should keep open
   My heavy eyelids to the weary night?
Dost thou desire my slumbers should be broken,
   While shadows, like to thee, do mock my sight?
Is it thy spirit that thou send'st from thee
   So far from home, into my deeds to pry;
To find out shames and idle hours in me,
   The scope and tenour of thy jealousy?
O no! thy love, though much, is not so great;
   It is my love that keeps mine eye awake;

---

[39] *whe'r*] i. e. whether.
[40] *main of light*] "i. e. the great body of light. So the *main* of waters."

Mine own true love that doth my rest defeat,
　To play the watchman ever for thy sake:
　　For thee watch I, whilst thou dost wake
　　　elsewhere,
　From me far off, with others all-too-near.

LXII

Sin of self-love possesseth all mine eye,
　And all my soul, and all my every part;
And for this sin there is no remedy,
　It is so grounded inward in my heart.
Methinks no face so gracious[41] is as mine,
　No shape so true, no truth of such account,
And for myself mine own worth do define,
　As I all other in all worths surmount.
But when my glass shows me myself indeed,
　Beated and chopp'd with tann'd antiquity,
Mine own self-love quite contrary I read,
　Self so self-loving were iniquity.
　　'Tis thee (myself) that for myself I praise,
　　Painting my age with beauty of thy days.

LXIII

Against my love shall be, as I am now,
　With time's injurious hand crush'd and o'erworn;
When hours have drain'd his blood, and fill'd his brow
　With lines and wrinkles; when his youthful morn
Hath travell'd on to age's steepy night;
　And all those beauties, whereof now he's king,
Are vanishing or vanish'd out of sight,
　Stealing away the treasure of his spring;
For such a time do I now fortify
　Against confounding age's cruel knife,

41 *gracious*] i. e. beautiful.

That he shall never cut from memory
   My sweet love's beauty, though my lover's life.
      His beauty shall in these black lines be seen,
      And they shall live, and he in them still green

LXIV

When I have seen by Time's fell hand defac'd
   The rich-proud cost of outworn buried age;
When sometime lofty towers I see down-ras'd,
   And brass eternal, slave to mortal rage;
When I have seen the hungry ocean gain
   Advantage on the kingdom of the shore,
And the firm soil win of the wat'ry main,
   Increasing store with loss, and loss with store;
When I have seen such interchange of state,
   Or state itself confounded to decay;
Ruin hath taught me thus to ruminate—
   That time will come and take my love away.
      This thought is as a death, which cannot choose
      But weep to have that which it fears to lose.

LXV

Since brass, nor stone, nor earth, nor boundless sea,
   But sad mortality o'ersways their power,
How with this rage shall beauty hold a plea,
   Whose action is no stronger than a flower?
O, how shall summer's honey breath hold out
   Against the wreckful siege of battering days,
When rocks impregnable are not so stout,
   Nor gates of steel so strong, but time decays?
O fearful meditation! where, alack!
   Shall time's best jewel from time's chest lie hid?
Or what strong hand can hold his swift foot back?
   Or who his spoil of beauty can forbid?

O none, unless this miracle have might,
That in black ink my love may still shine bright.

LXVI

Tir'd with all these, for restful death I cry,—
    As, to behold desert a beggar born,
And needy nothing trimm'd in jollity,
    And purest faith unhappily forsworn,
And gilded honour shamefully misplac'd,
    And maiden virtue rudely strumpeted,
And right perfection wrongfully disgrac'd,
    And strength by limping sway disabled,
And art made tongue-tied by authority,
    And folly (doctor-like) controlling skill,
And simple truth miscall'd simplicity,
    And captive good attending captain ill:
        Tir'd with all these, from these would I be gone,
        Save that, to die, I leave my love alone.

LXVII

Ah! wherefore with infection should he live,
    And with his presence grace impiety,
That sin by him advantage should achieve,
    And lace[42] itself with his society?
Why should false painting imitate his cheek,
    And steal dead seeing of his living hue?
Why should poor beauty indirectly seek
    Roses of shadow, since his rose is true?
Why should he live now nature bankrupt is,
    Beggar'd of blood to blush through lively veins?
For she hath no exchequer now but his,
    And proud of many, lives upon his gains.
        O, him she stores, to show what wealth she had,
        In days long since, before these last so bad.

42 *lace*] i. e. embellish.

LXVIII

Thus is his cheek the map of days outworn,
    When beauty liv'd and died as flowers do now,
Before these bastard signs of fair were borne,
    Or durst inhabit on a living brow;
Before the golden tresses of the dead,
    The right of sepulchres, were shorn away,
To live a second life on second head,
    Ere beauty's dead fleece made another gay:
In him those holy antique hours are seen,
    Without all ornament, itself, and true,
Making no summer of another's green,
    Robbing no old to dress his beauty new;
        And him as for a map doth nature store,
        To show false art what beauty was of yore.

LXIX

Those parts of thee that the world's eye doth view,
    Want nothing that the thought of hearts can mend.
All tongues (the voice of souls) give thee that due,
    Uttering bare truth, even so as foes commend.
Thine outward thus with outward praise is crown'd;
    But those same tongues that give thee so thine own,
In other accents do this praise confound,
    By seeing farther than the eye hath shown.
They look into the beauty of thy mind,
    And that, in guess, they measure by thy deeds;
Then (churls) their thoughts, although their eyes were
        kind,
    To thy fair flower add the rank smell of weeds:
        But why thy odour matcheth not thy show,
        The solve[43] is this,—that thou dost common
        grow.

[43] *solve*] i. e. solution; so Malone: Steevens proposes to read "*sole*."—
The old copy has "*solye*."

LXX

That thou art blam'd shall not be thy defect,
    For slander's mark was ever yet the fair;
The ornament of beauty is suspect,[44]
    A crow that flies in heaven's sweetest air.
So thou be good, slander doth but approve
    Thy worth the greater, being woo'd of time;
For canker vice the sweetest buds doth love,
    And thou present'st a pure unstained prime.
Thou hast pass'd by the ambush of young days,
    Either not assail'd, or victor being charg'd;
Yet this thy praise cannot be so thy praise,
    To tie up envy, evermore enlarg'd:
        If some suspect of ill mask'd not thy show,
        Then thou alone kingdoms of hearts should'st
           owe.[45]

LXXI

No longer mourn for me when I am dead,
    Than you shall hear the surly sullen bell
Give warning to the world that I am fled
    From this vile world, with vilest worms to dwell:
Nay, if you read this line, remember not
    The hand that writ it; for I love you so,
That I in your sweet thoughts would be forgot,
    If thinking on me then should make you woe.
O if (I say) you look upon this verse,
    When I perhaps compounded am with clay,
Do not so much as my poor name rehearse;
    But let your love even with my life decay:
        Lest the wise world should look into your moan,
        And mock you with me after I am gone.

[44] *suspect*] i. e. suspicion.
[45] *owe*] i. e. own, possess.

LXXII

O, lest the world should task you to recite
    What merit liv'd in me, that you should love
After my death,—dear love, forget me quite,
    For you in me can nothing worthy prove;
Unless you would devise some virtuous lie,
    To do more for me than mine own desert,
And hang more praise upon deceased I
    Than niggard truth would willingly impart:
O, lest your true love may seem false in this,
    That you for love speak well of me untrue,
My name be buried where my body is,
    And live no more to shame nor me nor you.
        For I am sham'd by that which I bring forth,
        And so should you, to love things nothing worth.

LXXIII

That time of year thou may'st in me behold
    When yellow leaves, or none, or few, do hang
Upon those boughs which shake against the cold,
    Bare ruin'd choirs, where late the sweet birds sang.
In me thou seest the twilight of such day,
    As after sunset fadeth in the west,
Which by and by black night doth take away,
    Death's second self, that seals up all in rest.
In me thou seest the glowing of such fire,
    That on the ashes of his youth doth lie,
As the death-bed whereon it must expire,
    Consum'd with that which it was nourish'd by.
        This thou perceiv'st, which makes thy love more
           strong,
        To love that well which thou must leave ere
           long:

LXXIV

But be contented: when that fell arrest
    Without all bail shall carry me away,
My life hath in this line some interest,
    Which for memorial still with thee shall stay.
When thou reviewest this, thou dost review
    The very part was consecrate to thee.
The earth can have but earth, which is his due;
    My spirit is thine, the better part of me:
So then thou hast but lost the dregs of life,
    The prey of worms, my body being dead;
The coward conquest of a wretch's knife,
    Too base of thee to be remembered.
        The worth of that, is that which it contains,
        And that is this, and this with thee remains.

LXXV

So are you to my thoughts, as food to life,
    Or as sweet-season'd showers are to the ground;
And for the peace of you I hold such strife
    As 'twixt a miser and his wealth is found;
Now proud as an enjoyer, and anon
    Doubting the filching age will steal his treasure;
Now counting best to be with you alone,
    Then better'd that the world may see my pleasure:
Sometime, all full with feasting on your sight,
    And by and by clean starved for a look;
Possessing or pursuing no delight,
    Save what is had or must from you be took.
        Thus do I pine and surfeit day by day,
        Or gluttoning on all, or all away.

LXXVI

Why is my verse so barren of new pride?
    So far from variation or quick change?

Why, with the time, do I not glance aside
    To new-found methods and to compounds strange?
Why write I still all one, ever the same,
    And keep invention in a noted weed,
That every word doth almost tell my name,
    Showing their birth, and where they did proceed?
O know, sweet love, I always write of you,
    And you and love are still my argument;
So all my best is dressing old words new,
    Spending again what is already spent:
        For as the sun is daily new and old,
        So is my love still telling what is told.

LXXVII

Thy glass will show thee how thy beauties wear,
    Thy dial how thy precious minutes waste;
The vacant leaves thy mind's imprint will bear,
    And of this book this learning may'st thou taste.
The wrinkles which thy glass will truly show,
    Of mouthed graves will give thee memory;
Thou by thy dial's shady stealth may'st know
    Time's thievish progress to eternity.
Look, what thy memory cannot contain,
    Commit to these waste blanks, and thou shalt find
Those children nurs'd, deliver'd from thy brain,
    To take a new acquaintance of thy mind.
        These offices, so oft as thou wilt look,
        Shall profit thee, and much enrich thy book.

LXXVIII

So oft have I invok'd thee for my muse,
    And found such fair assistance in my verse,
As every alien pen hath got my use,
    And under thee their poesy disperse.

Thine eyes, that taught the dumb on high to sing,
    And heavy ignorance aloft to fly,
Have added feathers to the learned's wing,
    And given grace a double majesty.
Yet be most proud of that which I compile,
    Whose influence is thine, and born of thee:
In others' works thou dost but mend the style,
    And arts with thy sweet graces graced be;
        But thou art all my art, and dost advance
        As high as learning my rude ignorance.

LXXIX

Whilst I alone did call upon thy aid,
    My verse alone had all thy gentle grace;
But now my gracious numbers are decay'd,
    And my sick muse doth give another place.
I grant, sweet love, thy lovely argument
    Deserves the travail of a worthier pen;
Yet what of thee thy poet doth invent,
    He robs thee of, and pays it thee again.
He lends thee virtue, and he stole that word
    From thy behaviour; beauty doth he give,
And found it in thy cheek; he can afford
    No praise to thee but what in thee doth live.
        Then thank him not for that which he doth say,
        Since what he owes thee thou thyself dost pay.

LXXX

O, how I faint when I of you do write,
    Knowing a better spirit[47] doth use your name,
And in the praise thereof spends all his might,
    To make me tongue-tied, speaking of your fame!
But since your worth (wide, as the ocean is,)
    The humble as the proudest sail doth bear,

[47] *a better spirit*] has been supposed to mean Spenser.

My saucy bark, inferior far to his,
    On your broad main doth wilfully appear.
Your shallowest help will hold me up afloat,
    Whilst he upon your soundless deep doth ride;
Or, being wreck'd, I am a worthless boat,
    He of tall building, and of goodly pride:
        Then if he thrive, and I be cast away,
        The worst was this;—my love was my decay.

LXXXI

Or I shall live your epitaph to make,
    Or you survive when I in earth am rotten;
From hence your memory death cannot take,
    Although in me each part will be forgotten.
Your name from hence immortal life shall have,
    Though I, once gone, to tell the world must die:
The earth can yield me but a common grave,
    When you entombed in men's eyes shall lie.
Your monument shall be my gentle verse,
    Which eyes not yet created shall o'er-read;
And tongues to be, your being shall rehearse,
    When all the breathers of this world are dead;
        You still shall live (such virtue hath my pen,)
        Where breath most breathes,—even in the
          mouths of men.

LXXXII

I grant thou wert not married to my muse,
    And therefore may'st without attaint o'erlook
The dedicated words which writers use
    Of their fair subject, blessing every book.
Thou art as fair in knowledge as in hue,
    Finding thy worth a limit past my praise;
And therefore art enforc'd to seek anew
    Some fresher stamp of the time-bettering days.

93

And do so, love; yet when they have devis'd
   What strained touches rhetorick can lend,
Thou truly fair wert truly sympathiz'd
   In true plain words, by thy true-telling friend;
      And their gross painting might be better us'd
      Where cheeks need blood; in thee it is abus'd.

LXXXIII

I never saw that you did painting need,
   And therefore to your fair[48] no painting set.
I found, or thought I found, you did exceed
   The barren tender of a poet's debt:
And therefore have I slept in your report,
   That you yourself, being extant, well might show
How far a modern[49] quill doth come too short,
   Speaking of worth, what worth in you doth grow.
This silence for my sin you did impute,
   Which shall be most my glory, being dumb;
For I impair not beauty being mute,
   When others would give life, and bring a tomb.
      There lives more life in one of your fair eyes
      Than both your poets can in praise devise.

LXXXIV

Who is it that says most? which can say more,
   Than this rich praise,—that you alone are you?
In whose confine immured is the store
   Which should example where your equal grew.
Lean penury within that pen doth dwell,
   That to his subject lends not some small glory;
But he that writes of you, if he can tell
   That you are you, so dignifies his story,

48 *fair*] i. e. beauty.
49 *modern*] i. e. common, worthless.

94

Let him but copy what in you is writ,
　　Not making worse what nature made so clear,
And such a counter part shall fame his wit,
　　Making his style admired every where.
　　　　You to your beauteous blessings add a curse,
　　　　Being fond on praise, which makes your praises
　　　　　worse.

LXXXV

My tongue-tied muse in manners holds her still,
　　While comments of your praise, richly compil'd,
Reserve[50] their character with golden quill,
　　And precious phrase by all the muses fil'd.
I think good thoughts, while others write good words,
　　And, like unletter'd clerk, still cry *Amen*
To every hymn that able spirit affords,
　　In polish'd form of well-refin'd pen.
Hearing you prais'd, I say, *'tis so, 'tis true,*
　　And to the most of praise add something more;
But that is in my thought, whose love to you,
　　Though words come hindmost, holds his rank
　　　　before.
　　　　Then others for the breath of words respect,
　　　　Me for my dumb thoughts, speaking in effect.

LXXXVI

Was it the proud full sail of his great verse,
　　Bound for the prize of all-too-precious you,
That did my ripe thoughts in my brain inhearse,
　　Making their tomb the womb wherein they grew?
Was it his spirit, by spirits taught to write
　　Above a mortal pitch, that struck me dead?
No, neither he, nor his compeers by night
　　Giving him aid, my verse astonished.

[50] *Reserve*] i. e. preserve.

95

He, nor that affable familiar ghost
    Which nightly gulls him with intelligence,
As victors, of my silence cannot boast;
    I was not sick of any fear from thence.
        But when your countenance fil'd[51] up his line,
        Then lack'd I matter; that enfeebled mine.

LXXXVII

Farewell! thou art too dear for my possessing,
    And like enough thou know'st thy estimate:
The charter of thy worth gives thee releasing;
    My bonds in thee are all determinate.[52]
For how do I hold thee but by thy granting?
    And for that riches where is my deserving?
The cause of this fair gift in me is wanting,
    And so my patent back again is swerving.
Thyself thou gav'st, thy own worth then now knowing,
    Or me, to whom thou gav'st it, else mistaking;
So thy great gift, upon misprison growing,
    Comes home again, on better judgment making.
        Thus have I had thee, as a dream doth flatter,
        In sleep a king, but waking, no such matter.

LXXXVIII

When thou shalt be dispos'd to set me light,
    And place my merit in the eye of Scorn,
Upon thy side against myself I'll fight,
    And prove thee virtuous, though thou art forsworn.
With mine own weakness being best acquainted,
    Upon thy part I can set down a story
Of faults conceal'd, wherein I am attainted;
    That thou, in losing me, shalt win much glory:
And I by this will be a gainer too;
    For bending all my loving thoughts on thee,

51 *fil'd*] i. e. polished.   52 *determinate*] i. e. ended, out of date.

The injuries that to myself I do,
    Doing thee vantage, double-vantage me.
        Such is my love, to thee I so belong,
        That for thy right myself will bear all wrong.

LXXXIX

Say that thou didst forsake me for some fault,
    And I will comment upon that offence:
Speak of my lameness, and I straight will halt;
    Against thy reasons making no defence.
Thou canst not, love, disgrace me half so ill,
    To set a form upon desired change,
As I'll myself disgrace: knowing thy will,
    I will acquaintance strangle, and look strange;
Be absent from thy walks; and in my tongue
    Thy sweet-beloved name no more shall dwell;
Lest I (too much profane) should do it wrong,
    And haply of our old acquaintance tell.
        For thee, against myself I'll vow debate,
        For I must ne'er love him whom thou dost hate.

XC

Then hate me when thou wilt; if ever, now;
    Now while the world is bent my deeds to cross,
Join with the spite of fortune, make me bow,
    And do not drop in for an after-loss:
Ah! do not, when my heart hath scap'd this sorrow,
    Come in the rearward of a conquer'd woe;
Give not a windy night a rainy morrow,
    To linger out a purpos'd overthrow.
If thou wilt leave me, do not leave me last,
    When other petty griefs have done their spite,
But in the onset come; so shall I taste
    At first the very worst of fortune's might;

And other strains of woe, which now seem woe,
Compar'd with loss of thee will not seem so.

XCI

Some glory in their birth, some in their skill,
    Some in their wealth, some in their body's force;
Some in their garments, though new-fangled ill;
    Some in their hawks and hounds, some in their
        horse;
And every humour hath his adjunct pleasure,
    Wherein it finds a joy above the rest;
But these particulars are not my measure,
    All these I better in one general best.
Thy love is better than high birth to me,
    Richer than wealth, prouder than garments' cost,
Of more delight than hawks or horses be;
    And having thee, of all men's pride I boast.
        Wretched in this alone, that thou may'st take
        All this away, and me most wretched make.

XCII

But do thy worst to steal thyself away,
    For term of life thou art assured mine;
And life no longer than thy love will stay,
    For it depends upon that love of thine.
Then need I not to fear the worst of wrongs,
    When in the least of them my life hath end.
I see a better state to me belongs
    Than that which on thy humour doth depend.
Thou canst not vex me with inconstant mind,
    Since that my life on thy revolt doth lie.
O what a happy title do I find,
    Happy to have thy love, happy to die!
        But what's so blessed-fair that fears no blot?—
        Thou may'st be false, and yet I know it not:

XCIII

So shall I live, supposing thou art true,
    Like a deceived husband; so love's face
May still seem love to me, though alter'd-new;
    Thy looks with me, thy heart in other place:
For there can live no hatred in thine eye,
    Therefore in that I cannot know thy change.
In many's looks the false heart's history
    Is writ, in moods and frowns and wrinkles strange;
But heaven in thy creation did decree,
    That in thy face sweet love should ever dwell;
Whate'er thy thoughts or thy heart's workings be,
    Thy looks should nothing thence but sweetness tell.
        How like Eve's apple doth thy beauty grow,
        If thy sweet virtue answer not thy show!

XCIV

They that have power to hurt and will do none,
    That do not do the thing they most do show,
Who, moving others, are themselves as stone,
    Unmoved, cold, and to temptation slow;
They rightly do inherit heaven's graces,
    And husband nature's riches from expence;
They are the lords and owners of their faces,
    Others but stewards of their excellence.
The summer's flower is to the summer sweet,
    Though to itself it only live and die;
But if that flower with base infection meet,
    The basest weed out-braves his dignity:
        For sweetest things turn sourest by their deeds;
        Lilies that fester smell far worse than weeds.

XCV

How sweet and lovely dost thou make the shame
    Which, like a canker in the fragrant rose,

100

Doth spot the beauty of thy budding name!
 O, in what sweets dost thou thy sins enclose!
That tongue that tells the story of thy days,
 Making lascivious comments on thy sport,
Cannot dispraise but in a kind of praise;
 Naming thy name blesses an ill report.
O what a mansion have those vices got,
 Which for their habitation chose out thee!
Where beauty's veil doth cover every blot,
  And all things turn to fair, that eyes can see!
   Take heed, dear heart, of this large privilege;
   The hardest knife ill-us'd doth lose his edge.

XCVI

Some say, thy fault is youth, some wantonness;
 Some say, thy grace is youth and gentle sport;
Both grace and faults are lov'd of more and less:
 Thou mak'st faults graces that to thee resort.
As on the finger of a throned queen
 The basest jewel will be well esteem'd;
So are those errors that in thee are seen,
 To truths translated, and for true things deem'd.
How many lambs might the stern wolf betray,
 If like a lamb he could his looks translate!
How many gazers might'st thou lead away,
 If thou would'st use the strength of all thy state!
  But do not so; I love thee in such sort,
  As thou being mine, mine is thy good report.

XCVII

How like a winter hath my absence been
 From thee, the pleasure of the fleeting year!
What freezings have I felt, what dark days seen!
 What old December's bareness every where!

101

And yet this time remov'd[53] was summer's time;
    The teeming autumn, big with rich increase,
Bearing the wanton burden of the prime,
    Like widow'd wombs after their lord's decease:
Yet this abundant issue seem'd to me
    But hope of orphans, and unfather'd fruit;
For summer and his pleasures wait on thee,
    And thou away, the very birds are mute;
        Or, if they sing, 'tis with so dull a cheer,
        That leaves look pale, dreading the winter's
        near.

XCVIII

From you have I been absent in the spring,
    When proud-pied April, dress'd in all his trim,
Hath put a spirit of youth in every thing
    That heavy Saturn laugh'd and leap'd with him.
Yet nor the lays of birds, nor the sweet smell
    Of different flowers in odour and in hue,
Could make me any summer's story tell,
    Or from their proud lap pluck them where they
        grew:
Nor did I wonder at the lilies white,
    Nor praise the deep vermilion in the rose;
They were but sweet, but figures of delight,
    Drawn after you, you pattern of all those.
        Yet seem'd it winter still, and, you away,
        As with your shadow I with these did play:

XCIX

The forward violet thus did I chide;—
    Sweet thief, whence didst thou steal thy sweet that
        smells,

[53] *this time remov'd*] "i. e. this time in which I was remote or absent from thee." MALONE.

If not from my love's breath? The purple pride
    Which on thy soft cheek for complexion dwells,
In my love's veins thou hast too grossly dy'd.
    The lily I condemned for thy hand,
And buds of marjoram had stolen thy hair:
    The roses fearfully on thorns did stand,
One blushing shame, another white despair;
    A third, nor red nor white, had stolen of both,
And to his robbery had annex'd thy breath;
    But for his theft, in pride of all his growth
A vengeful canker eat him up to death.
        More flowers I noted, yet I none could see,
        But sweet or colour it had stolen from thee.

c

Where art thou, Muse, that thou forget'st so long
    To speak of that which gives thee all thy might?
Spend'st thou thy fury on some worthless song,
    Darkening thy power, to lend base subjects light?
Return, forgetful Muse, and straight redeem
    In gentle numbers time so idly spent;
Sing to the ear that doth thy lays esteem,
    And gives thy pen both skill and argument.
Rise, restive Muse, my love's sweet face survey,
    If Time have any wrinkle graven there;
If any, be a satire to decay,
    And make Time's spoils despised every where.
        Give my love fame faster than Time wastes life;
        So thou prevent'st[54] his scythe, and crooked
        knife.

CI

O truant Muse, what shall be thy amends,
    For thy neglect of truth in beauty dy'd?

[54] *So thou prevent'st his scythe,* &c.] "i. e. so by anticipation thou hinderest the destructive effects of his weapon." STEEVENS.

103

Both truth and beauty on my love depends;
   So dost thou too, and therein dignify'd.
Make answer, Muse: wilt thou not haply say,
   Truth needs no colour with his colour fix'd,
Beauty no pencil, beauty's truth to lay;
   But best is best, if never intermix'd?—
Because he needs no praise, wilt thou be dumb?
   Excuse not silence so; for it lies in thee
To make him much outlive a gilded tomb,
   And to be prais'd of ages yet to be.
      Then do thy office, Muse; I teach thee how
      To make him seem long hence as he shows now.

CII

My love is strengthen'd, though more weak in seeming;
   I love not less, though less the show appear;
That love is merchandiz'd, whose rich esteeming
   The owner's tongue doth publish every where.
Our love was new, and then but in the spring,
   When I was wont to greet it with my lays;
As Philomel in summer's front doth sing,
   And stops his pipe in growth of riper days:
Not that the summer is less pleasant now
   Than when her mournful hymns did hush the night,
But that wild musick burthens every bough,
   And sweets grown common lose their dear delight.
      Therefore, like her, I sometime hold my tongue,
      Because I would not dull you with my song.

CIII

Alack! what poverty my muse brings forth,
   That having such a scope to show her pride,
The argument, all bare, is of more worth,
   Than when it hath my added praise beside.

O blame me not if I no more can write!
    Look in your glass, and there appears a face
That over-goes my blunt invention quite,
    Dulling my lines, and going me disgrace.
Were it not sinful then, striving to mend,
    To mar the subject that before was well?
For to no other pass my verses tend,
    Than of your graces and your gifts to tell;
        And more, much more, than in my verse can sit,
        Your own glass shows you, when you look in it.

CIV

To me, fair friend, you never can be old,
    For as you were, when first your eye I ey'd,
Such seems your beauty still. Three winters cold
    Have from the forests shook three summers' pride;
Three beauteous springs to yellow autumn turn'd,
    In process of the seasons have I seen,
Three April perfumes in three hot Junes burn'd,
    Since first I saw you fresh which yet are green.
Ah! yet doth beauty, like a dial hand,
    Steal from his figure, and no pace perceiv'd;
So your sweet hue, which methinks still doth stand,
    Hath motion, and mine eye may be deceiv'd.
        For fear of which, hear this, thou age unbred,
        Ere you were born, was beauty's summer dead.

CV

Let not my love be call'd idolatry,
    Nor my beloved as an idol show,
Since all alike my songs and praises be,
    To one, of one, still such, and ever so.
Kind is my love to-day, to-morrow kind,
    Still constant in a wondrous excellence:

105

Therefore my verse to constancy confin'd,
    One thing expressing, leaves out difference.
Fair, kind, and true, is all my argument,
    Fair, kind, and true, varying to other words;
And in this change is my invention spent,
      Three themes in one, which wondrous scope affords.
      Fair, kind, and true, have often liv'd alone,
      Which three, till now, never kept seat in one.

CVI

When in the chronicle of wasted time
    I see descriptions of the fairest wights,
And beauty making beautiful old rhyme,
    In praise of ladies dead, and lovely knights,
Then in the blazon of sweet beauty's best,
    Of hand, of foot, of lip, of eye, of brow,
I see their antique pen would have express'd
    Even such a beauty as you master now.
So all their praises are but prophecies
    Of this our time, all you prefiguring;
And, for they look'd but with divining eyes,
    They had not skill enough your worth to sing:
      For we, which now behold these present days,
      Have eyes to wonder, but lack tongues to praise.

CVII

Not mine own fears, nor the prophetic soul
    Of the wide world dreaming on things to come,
Can yet the lease of my true love control,
    Suppos'd as forfeit to a confin'd doom.
The mortal moon hath her eclipse endur'd,
    And the sad augurs mock their own presage;
Incertainties now crown themselves assur'd,
    And peace proclaims olives of endless age.

106

Now with the drops of this most balmy time
    My love looks fresh, and death to me subscribes,[55]
Since spite of him I'll live in this poor rhyme,
    While he insults o'er dull and speechless tribes.
      And thou in this shalt find thy monument,
      When tyrants' crests and tombs of brass are
        spent.

CVIII

What's in the brain that ink may character,
    Which hath not figur'd to thee my true spirit?
What's new to speak, what new to register,
    That may express my love, or thy dear merit?
Nothing, sweet boy; but yet, like prayers divine,
    I must each day say o'er the very same;
Counting no old thing old, thou mine, I thine,
    Even as when first I hallow'd thy fair name.
So that eternal love in love's fresh case
    Weighs not the dust and injury of age,
Nor gives to necessary wrinkles place,
    But makes antiquity for aye his page;
      Finding the first conceit of love there bred,
      Where time and outward form would show it
        dead.

CIX

O, never say that I was false of heart,
    Though absence seem'd my flame to qualify!
As easy might I from myself depart,
    As from my soul which in thy breast doth lie:
That is my home of love: if I have rang'd,
    Like him that travels, I return again;
Just to the time, not with the time exchang'd,—
    So that myself bring water for my stain.

[55] *subscribes*] i. e. submits.

107

Never believe, though in my nature reign'd
 All frailties that besiege all kinds of blood,
That it could so preposterously be stain'd,
 To leave for nothing all thy sum of good;
  For nothing this wide universe I call,
  Save thou, my rose; in it thou art my all.

CX

Alas, 'tis true, I have gone here and there,
 And made myself a motley to the view,[57]
Gor'd mine own thoughts, sold cheap what is most dear,
 Made old offences of affections new.
Most true it is, that I have look'd on truth
 Askance and strangely; but, by all above,
These blenches[58] gave my heart another youth,
 And worse essays prov'd thee my best of love.
Now all is done, save what shall have no end:
 Mine appetite I never more will grind
On newer proof, to try an older friend,
 A God in love, to whom I am confin'd.
  Then give me welcome, next my heaven the best,
  Even to thy pure and most most loving breast.

CXI

O, for my sake do you with fortune chide,
 The guilty goddess of my harmful deeds,
That did not better for my life provide,
 Than publick means, which publick manner breeds.
Thence comes it that my name receives a brand,
 And almost thence my nature is subdu'd
To what it works in, like the dyer's hand:
 Pity me then, and wish I were renew'd;

57 *And made myself a motley to the view*] i. e. seemed like a fool; whose dress used to be *motley*.
58 *blenches*] i. e. starts, deviations.

Whilst, like a willing patient, I will drink
    Potions of eysell,[59] 'gainst my strong infection;
No bitterness that I will bitter think,
    Nor double penance, to correct correction.
        Pity me then, dear friend, and I assure ye,
        Even that your pity is enough to cure me.

CXII

Your love and pity doth the impression fill
    Which vulgar scandal stamp'd upon my brow;
For what care I who calls me well or ill,
    So you o'er-green my bad, my good allow?[60]
You are my all-the-world, and I must strive
    To know my shame and praises from your tongue;
None else to me,[61] nor I to none alive,
    That my steel'd sense or changes, right or wrong.
In so profound abysm I throw all care
    Of other's voices, that my adder's sense
To critick and to flatterer stopped are.
        Mark how with my neglect I do dispense:—
        You are so strongly in my purpose bred,
        That all the world besides methinks are[62] dead.

CXIII

Since I left you, mine eye is in my mind,
    And that which governs me to go about,
Doth part his functions, and is partly blind,
    Seems seeing, but effectually is out;
For it no form delivers to the heart
    Of bird, of flower, or shape, which it doth latch;[63]

59 *eysell*] i. e. vinegar.
60 *allow*] i. e. approve.
61 *None else to me*, &c.] "the meaning seems to be—you are the only person who has power to change my stubborn resolution, either to what is right or to what is wrong." STEEVENS.
62 *are*] the old copy has "*y'are*" a common abbreviation of *you are*, not of *they are*, as Malone strangely supposes.
63 *latch*] i. e. lay hold of.

Of his quick objects hath the mind no part,
 Nor his own vision holds what it doth catch;
For if it see the rud'st or gentlest sight,
 The most sweet favour,[64] or deformed'st creature,
The mountain or the sea, the day or night,
 The crow, or dove, it shapes them to your feature.
  Incapable of more, replete with you,
  My most true mind thus maketh mine untrue.[65]

CXIV

Or whether doth my mind, being crown'd with you,
 Drink up the monarch's plague, this flattery,
Or whether shall I say mine eye saith true,
 And that your love taught it this alchymy,
To make of monsters and things indigest,
 Such cherubins as your sweet self resemble,
Creating every bad a perfect best,
 As fast as objects to his beams assemble?
O, 'tis the first; 'tis flattery in my seeing,
 And my great mind most kingly drinks it up:
Mine eye well knows what with his gust is 'greeing,
 And to his palate doth prepare the cup:
  If it be poison'd, 'tis the lesser sin
  That mine eye loves it, and doth first begin.

CXV

Those lines that I before have writ, do lie,
 Even those that said I could not love you dearer;
Yet then my judgment knew no reason why
 My most full flame should afterwards burn clearer.

64 *favour*] i. e. countenance.

65 *My most true mind thus maketh mine untrue*] "the word *untrue* is used as a substantive. 'The sincerity of my affection is the cause of my untruth;' i. e. of my not seeing objects truly, such as they appear to the rest of mankind." MALONE.

But reckoning time, whose million'd accidents
    Creep in 'twixt vows, and change decrees of kings,
Tan sacred beauty, blunt the sharp'st intents,
    Divert strong minds to the course of altering things;
Alas! why, fearing of time's tyranny,
    Might I not then say, *now I love you best,*
When I was certain o'er incertainty,
    Crowning the present, doubting of the rest?
        Love is a babe; then might I not say so,
        To give full growth to that which still doth
            grow?

CXVI

Let me not to the marriage of true minds
    Admit impediments. Love is not love
Which alters when it alteration finds,
    Or bends with the remover to remove:
O no; it is an ever-fixed mark,
    That looks on tempests, and is never shaken;
It is the star to every wandering bark,
    Whose worth's unknown, although his height be
        taken.
Love's not Time's fool, though rosy lips and cheeks
    Within his bending sickle's compass come;
Love alters not with his brief hours and weeks,
    But bears it out even to the edge of doom.
        If this be error, and upon me prov'd,
        I never writ, nor no man ever lov'd.

CXVII

Accuse me thus; that I have scanted all
    Wherein I should your great deserts repay;
Forgot upon your dearest love to call,
    Whereto all bonds do tie me day by day;

111

That I have frequent been with unknown minds,
    And given to time your own dear-purchas'd right;
That I have hoisted sail to all the winds
    Which should transport me farthest from your
        sight.
Book both my wilfulness and errors down,
    And on just proof, surmise accumulate,
Bring me within the level of your frown,
    But shoot not at me in your waken'd hate:
        Since my appeal says, I did strive to prove
        The constancy and virtue of your love.

CXVIII

Like as, to make our appetites more keen,
    With eager[66] compounds we our palate urge:
As, to prevent our maladies unseen,
    We sicken to shun sickness, when we purge;
Even so, being full of your ne'er-cloying sweetness,
    To bitter sauces did I frame my feeding,
And, sick of welfare, found a kind of meetness
    To be diseas'd, ere that there was true needing.
Thus policy in love, to anticipate
    The ills that were not, grew to faults assured,
And brought to medicine a healthful state,
    Which, rank of goodness, would by ill be cured
        But thence I learn, and find the lesson true,
        Drugs poison him that so fell sick of you.

CXIX

What potions have I drunk of Syren tears,
    Distill'd from limbecs foul as hell within,
Applying fears to hopes, and hopes to fears,
    Still losing when I saw myself to win!

[66] *eager*] i. e. sour.

What wretched errors hath my heart committed,
  Whilst it hath thought itself so blessed never!
How have mine eyes[67] out of their spheres been fitted,
  In the distraction of this madding fever!
O benefit of ill! now I find true
  That better is by evil still made better;
And ruin'd love, when it is built anew,
  Grows fairer than at first, more strong, far greater.
    So I return rebuk'd to my content,
    And gain by ill thrice more than I have spent.

CXX

That you were once unkind, befriends me now,
  And for that sorrow, which I then did feel,
Needs must I under my transgression bow,
  Unless my nerves were brass or hammer'd steel.
For if you were by my unkindness shaken,
  As I by yours, you have pass'd a hell of time:
And I, a tyrant, have no leisure taken
  To weigh how once I suffer'd in your crime.
O that our night of woe might have remember'd[68]
  My deepest sense, how hard true sorrow hits,
And soon to you, as you to me, then tender'd
  The humble salve which wounded bosoms fits!
    But that your trespass now becomes a fee;
    Mine ransoms yours, and yours must ransom me.

CXXI

'Tis better to be vile, then vile esteem'd,
  When not to be receives reproach of being,
And the just pleasure lost, which is so deem'd
  Not by our feeling, but by others' seeing.

---

[67] *How have mine eyes, &c.*] "How have mine eyes been convulsed during the frantic *fits* of my feverous love!" MALONE.
[68] *remember'd*] i. e. reminded.

113

For why should others' false adulterate eyes
    Give salutation to my sportive blood?
Or on my frailties why are frailer spies,
    Which in their wills count bad what I think good?
No.—I am that I am; and they that level
    At my abuses, reckon up their own:
I may be straight, though they themselves be bevel;[69]
    By their rank thoughts my deeds must not be shown;
      Unless this general evil they maintain,—
      All men are bad, and in their badness reign.

CXXII

Thy gift, thy tables, are within my brain
    Full character'd with lasting memory,
Which shall above that idle rank remain,
    Beyond all date, even to eternity:
Or at the least so long as brain and heart
    Have faculty by nature to subsist;
Till each to raz'd oblivion yield his part
    Of thee, thy record never can be miss'd.
That poor retention could not so much hold,[70]
    Nor need I tallies, thy dear love to score;
Therefore to give them from me was I bold,
    To trust those tables that receive thee more:
      To keep an adjunct to remember thee,
      Were to import forgetfulness in me.

CXXIII

No! Time, thou shalt not boast that I do change:
    Thy pyramids built up with newer might

69 *bevel*] i. e. crooked. "In masonry and joinery [bevel is] a kind of square, one leg of which is frequently crooked, according to the sweep of an arch or vault." BUILDER'S DICT.

70 *That poor retention could not so much hold*] "*That poor retention* is the table-book given to him by his friend, incapable of *retaining*, or rather of containing, so much as the *tablet of the brain*." MALONE.

To me are nothing novel, nothing strange;
　　They are but dressings of a former sight.
Our dates are brief, and therefore we admire
　　What thou dost foist upon us that is old;
And rather make them born to our desire,
　　Than think that we before have heard them told.
Thy registers and thee I both defy,
　　Not wondering at the present nor the past;
For thy records and what we see do lie,
　　Made more or less by this continual haste;
　　　　This I do vow, and this shall ever be,
　　　　I will be true, despite thy scythe and thee:

CXXIV

If my dear love were but the child of state,
　　It might for fortune's bastard be unfather'd.
As subject to time's love, or to time's hate,
　　Weeds among weeds, or flowers with flowers
　　　　gather'd.
No, it was builded far from accident;
　　It suffers not in smiling pomp, nor falls
Under the blow of thralled discontent,
　　Whereto the inviting time our fashion calls:
It fears not policy, that heretick,
　　Which works on leases of short-number'd hours,
But all alone stands hugely politick,
　　That it nor grows with heat, nor drowns with
　　　　showers,
　　　　To this I witness call the fools of time,
　　　　Which die for goodness, who have liv'd for
　　　　crime.

CXXV

Were it aught to me I bore the canopy,
　　With my extern the outward honouring,

Or laid great bases for eternity,
    Which prove more short than waste or ruining?
Have I not seen dwellers on form and favour
    Lose all, and more, by paying too much rent,
For compound sweet foregoing simple savour,
    Pitiful thrivers, in their gazing spent?
No;—let me be obsequious in thy heart,
    And take thou my oblation, poor but free,
Which is not mix'd with seconds, knows no art
    But mutual render, only me for thee.
        Hence, thou suborn'd informer! a true soul,
        When most impeach'd, stands least in thy
          control.

CXXVI

O thou, my lovely boy, who in thy power
    Dost hold time's fickle glass, his sickle, hour;
Who has by waning grown, and therein show'st
    Thy lovers withering, as they sweet self grow'st!
If nature, sovereign mistress over wrack,
    As thou goest onwards, still will pluck thee back,
She keeps thee to this purpose, that her skill
    May time disgrace, and wretched minutes kill.
Yet fear her, O thou minion of her pleasure;
    She may detain, but not still keep her treasure:
        Her audit, though delay'd, answer'd must be,
        And her quietus is to render thee.

CXXVII

In the old age black was not counted fair,
    Or if it were, it bore not beauty's name;
But now is black beauty's successive heir,
    And beauty slander'd with a bastard shame:
For since each hand hath put on nature's power,
    Fairing the foul with art's false borrow'd face,

116

Sweet beauty hath no name, no holy hour,
    But is profan'd, if not lives in disgrace.
Therefore my mistress' eyes are raven black,
    Her eyes so suited; and they mourners seem[72]
At such, who not born fair, no beauty lack,
    Slandering creation with a false esteem:
        Yet so they mourn, becoming of their woe,
        That every tongue says, beauty should look so.

CXXVIII

How oft, when thou, my musick, musick play'st,
    Upon that blessed wood whose motion sounds
With thy sweet fingers, when thou gently sway'st
    The wiry concord that mine ear confounds,
Do I envy those jacks,[73] that nimble leap
    To kiss the tender inward of thy hand,
Whilst my poor lips, which should that harvest reap,
    At the wood's boldness by thee blushing stand!
To be so tickled, they would change their state
    And situation with those dancing chips,
O'er whom thy fingers walk with gentle gait,
    Making dead wood more bless'd than living lips.
        Since saucy jacks so happy are in this,
        Give them thy fingers, me thy lips to kiss.

CXXIX

The expence of spirit in a waste of shame
    Is lust in action; and till action, lust
Is perjur'd, murderous, bloody, full of blame,
    Savage, extreme, rude, cruel, not to trust;

[72] *and they mourners seem,* &c.] "They seem to mourn that those who are not born fair, are yet possessed of an artificial beauty, by which they pass for what they are not and thus dishonour nature by their imperfect imitation and false pretensions." MALONE.

[73] *jacks*] Of the virginal,—a musical instrument of the spinnet kind.

Enjoy'd no sooner, but despised straight;
   Past reason hunted; and no sooner had
Past reason hated, as a swallow'd bait,
   On purpose laid to make the taker mad:
Mad in pursuit, and in possession so;
   Had, having, and in quest to have, extreme;
A bliss in proof,—and prov'd, a very woe;
   Before, a joy propos'd; behind, a dream;
      All this the world well knows; yet none knows
      well
      To shun the heaven that leads men to this hell.

CXXX

My mistress' eyes are nothing like the sun;
   Coral is far more red than her lips' red:
If snow be white, why then her breasts are dun;
   If hairs be wires, black wires grow on her head.
I have seen roses damask'd, red and white,
   But no such roses see I in her cheeks;
And in some perfumes is there more delight
   Than in the breath that from my mistress reeks.
I love to hear her speak,—yet well I know
   That musick hath a far more pleasing sound;
I grant I never saw a goddess go,—
   My mistress, when she walks, treads on the ground;
      And yet by heaven, I think my love as rare
      As any she bely'd with false compare.

CXXXI

Thou art as tyrannous, so as thou art,
   As those whose beauties proudly make them cruel;
For well thou know'st to my dear doting heart
   Thou art the fairest and most precious jewel.
Yet, in good faith, some say that thee behold,
   Thy face hath not the power to make love groan:

To say they err, I dare not be so bold,
   Although I swear it to myself alone.
And, to be sure that is not false I swear,
   A thousand groans, but thinking of thy face
One on another's neck, do witness bear
   Thy black is fairest in my judgment's place.
     In nothing art thou black, save in thy deeds,
     And thence this slander, as I think, proceeds.

CXXXII

Thine eyes I love, and they, as pitying me,
   Knowing thy heart, torment me with disdain;
Have put on black, and loving mourners be,
   Looking with pretty ruth upon my pain.
And truly not the morning sun of heaven
   Better becomes the grey cheeks of the east,
Nor that full star that ushers in the even,
   Doth half that glory to the sober west,
As those two mourning eyes become thy face.
   O, let it then as well beseem thy heart
To mourn for me, since mourning doth thee grace,
   And suit thy pity like in every part.
     Then will I swear beauty herself is black,
     And all they foul that thy complexion lack.

CXXXIII

Beshrew that heart that makes my heart to groan
   For that deep wound it gives my friend and me!
Is't not enough to torture me alone,
   But slave to slavery my sweet'st friend must be?
Me from myself thy cruel eye hath taken,
   And my next self thou harder hast engross'd;
Of him, myself, and thee, I am forsaken;
   A torment thrice three-fold thus to be cross'd.

119

Prison my heart in thy steel bosom's ward,
But then my friend's heart let my poor heart bail;
Who e'er keeps me, let my heart be his guard;
Thou canst not then use rigour in my goal:
And yet thou wilt; for I, being pent in thee,
Perforce am thine, and all that is in me.

CXXXIV

So now I have confess'd that he is thine,
And I myself am mortgag'd to thy will;
Myself I'll forfeit, so that other mine
Thou wilt restore, to be my comfort still:
But thou wilt not, nor he will not be free,
For thou art covetous, and he is kind;
He learn'd but, surety-like, to write for me,
Under that bond that him as fast doth bind.
The statute of thy beauty thou wilt take,
Thou usurer, that put'st forth all to use,
And sue a friend, came debtor for my sake;
So him I lose through my unkind abuse.
Him have I lost; thou hast both him and me;
He pays the whole, and yet am I not free.

CXXXV

Whoever hath her wish, thou hast thy will,
And will to boot, and will in over-plus;
More than enough am I that vex thee still,
To thy sweet will making addition thus.
Wilt thou, whose will is large and spacious,
Not once vouchsafe to hide my will in thine?
Shall will in others seem right gracious,
And in my will no fair acceptance shine?
The sea, all water, yet receives rain still,
And in abundance addeth to his store;

So thou, being rich in will, add to thy will
　One will of mine, to make thy large will more.
　　Let no unkind, no fair beseechers kill;
　　Think all but one, and me in that one *Will*.

CXXXVI

If thy soul check thee that I come so near,
　Swear to thy blind soul that I was thy *Will*,
And will, thy soul knows, is admitted there;
　　Thus far for love, my love-suit, sweet, fulfill.
Will will fulfill the treasure of thy love,
　Ay, fill it full with wills, and my will one,
In things of great receipt with ease we prove;
　　Among a number one is reckon'd none.
Then in the number let me pass untold,
　Though in thy stores' account I one must be;
For nothing hold me, so it please thee hold
　　That nothing me, a something sweet to thee:
　　　Make but my name thy love, and love that still,
　　　And then thou lov'st me,—for my name is *Will*.

CXXXVII

Thou blind fool, Love, what dost thou to mine eyes,
　That they behold, and see not what they see?
They know what beauty is, see where it lies,
　　Yet what the best is, take the worst to be.
If eyes, corrupt by over-partial looks,
　Be anchor'd in the bay where all men ride,
Why of eyes' falsehood hast thou forged hooks,
　Whereto the judgment of my heart is ty'd?
Why should my heart think that a several plot,[75]
　　Which my heart knows the wide world's common
　　　　place?

[75] *a several plot*] *a several* was a term for an enclosed field, in opposition
to an open field or common.

121

Or mine eyes seeing this, say this is not,
　　To put fair truth upon so foul a face?
　　　　In things right true my heart and eyes have
　　　　　err'd,
　　　　And to this false page are they now transferr'd.

CXXXVIII

When my love swears that she is made of truth,
　　I do believe her, though I know she lies;
That she might think me some untutor'd youth,
　　Unlearned in the world's false subtilties.
Thus vainly thinking that she thinks me young,
　　Although she knows my days are past the best,
Simply I credit her false-speaking tongue;
　　On both sides thus is simple truth supprest.
But wherefore says she not, she is unjust?
　　And wherefore say not I, that I am old?
O, love's best habit is in seeming trust.
　　And age in love loves not to have years told:
　　　　Therefore I lie with her, and she with me,
　　　　And in our faults by lies we flatter'd be.

CXXXIX

O, call not me to justify the wrong,
　　That thy unkindness lays upon my heart;
Wound me not with thine eye, but with thy tongue;
　　Use power with power, and slay me not by art
Tell me thou lov'st elsewhere; but in my sight,
　　Dear heart, forbear to glance thine eye aside.
What need'st thou wound with cunning, when thy
　　　might
　　Is more than my o'erpress'd defence can 'bide?
Let me excuse thee: ah! my love well knows
　　Her pretty looks have been mine enemies;

And therefore from my face she turns my foes,
    That they elsewhere might dart their injuries:
        Yet do not so; but since I am near slain,
        Kill me out-right with looks, and rid my pain.

CXL

Be wise as thou art cruel; do not press
    My tongue-ty'd patience with too much disdain;
Lest sorrow lend me words, and words express
    The manner of my pity-wanting pain.
If I might teach thee wit, better it were,
    Though not to love, yet, love, to tell me so;
(As testy sick men, when their deaths be near,
    No news but health from their physicians know;)
For, if I should despair, I should grow mad,
    And in my madness might speak ill of thee:
Now this ill-wresting world is grown so bad,
    Mad slanderers by mad ears believed be.
        That I may not be so, nor thou bely'd,
        Bear thine eyes straight, though thy proud heart
           go wide.

CXLI

In faith I do not love thee with mine eyes,
    For they in thee a thousand errors note;
But 'tis my heart that loves what they despise,
    Who in despite of view is pleas'd to dote.
Nor are mine ears with thy tongue's tune delighted;
    Nor tender feeling, to base touches prone,
Nor taste nor smell, desire to be invited
    To my sensual feast with thee alone:
But my five wits, nor my five senses can
    Dissuade one foolish heart from serving thee,
Who leaves unsway'd the likeness of a man,

123

Thy proud heart's slave and vassal wretch to be:
  Only my plague thus far I count my gain,
  That she that makes me sin, awards me pain.

CXLII

Love is my sin, and thy dear virtue hate,
  Hate of my sin, grounded on sinful loving:
O, but with mine compare thou thine own state,
  And thou shalt find it merits not reproving;
Or if it do, not from those lips of thine,
  That have profan'd their scarlet ornaments,
And seal'd false bonds of love as oft as mine;
  Robb'd others' beds revenues of their rents.
Be it lawful I love thee, as thou lov'st those
  Whom thine eyes woo as mine importune thee:
Root pity in thy heart, that when it grows,
  Thy pity may deserve to pity'd be.
    If thou dost seek to have what thou dost hide,
    By self-example may'st thou be deny'd!

CXLIII

Lo, as a careful housewife runs to catch
  One of her feather'd creatures broke away,
Sets down her babe, and makes all swift dispatch
  In pursuit of the thing she would have stay;
Whilst her neglected child holds her in chace,
  Cries to catch her whose busy care is bent
To follow that which flies before her face,
  Not prizing her poor infant's discontent;
So run'st thou after that which flies from thee,
  Whilst I thy babe chace thee afar behind;
But if thou catch thy hope, turn back to me,
  And play the mother's part, kiss me, be kind:
    So will I pray that thou may'st have thy *Will,*
    If thou turn back, and my loud crying still.

124

CXLIV

Two loves I have of comfort and despair,
    While like two spirits do suggest[76] me still;
The better angel is a man right fair,
    The worser spirit a woman, colour'd ill.
To win me soon to hell, my female evil
    Tempteth my better angel from my side,
And would corrupt my saint to be a devil,
    Wooing his purity with her foul pride.
And whether that my angel be turn'd fiend,
    Suspect I may, yet not directly tell;
But being both from me, both to each friend,
    I guess one angel in another's hell.
        Yet this shall I ne'er know, but live in doubt,
        Till my bad angel fire my good one out.

CXLV

Those lips that Love's own hand did make,
    Breath'd forth the sound that said, *I hate,*
To me that languish'd for her sake:
    But when she saw my woeful state,
Straight in her heart did mercy come,
    Chiding that tongue, that ever sweet
Was us'd in giving gentle doom;
    And taught it thus anew to greet:
I hate she alter'd with an end,
    That follow'd it as gentle day
Doth follow night, who like a fiend
    From heaven to hell is flown away.
        I hate from hate away she threw,
        And sav'd my life, saying—*not you.*

[76] *suggest*] i. e. tempt.

CXLVI

Poor soul, the centre of my sinful earth,
    Fool'd by those rebel powers that thee array,
Why dost thou pine within and, suffer dearth,
    Painting thy outward walls so costly gay?
Why so large cost, having so short a lease,
    Dost thou upon thy fading mansion spend?
Shall worms, inheritors of this excess,
    Eat up thy charge? Is this thy body's end?
Then, soul, live thou upon thy servant's loss,
    And let that pine to aggravate thy store;
Buy terms divine in selling hours of dross;
    Within be fed, without be rich no more:
        So shalt thou feed on death, that feeds on men,
        And, death once dead, there's no more dying
          then.

CXLVII

My love is as a fever, longing still
    For that which longer nurseth the disease;
Feeding on that which doth preserve the ill,
    The uncertain sickly appetite to please.
My reason, the physician to my love,
    Angry that his prescriptions are not kept,
Hath left me, and I desperate now approve,
    Desire is death, which physic did except.
Past cure I am, now reason is past care,
    And frantic mad with evermore unrest;
My thoughts and my discourse as mad men's are,
    At random from the truth vainly express'd;
        For I have sworn thee fair, and thought thee
          bright,
        Who art as black as hell, as dark as night.

126

CXLVIII

O me! what eyes hath love put in my head,
    Which have no correspondence with true sight?
Or, if they have, where is my judgment fled,
    That censures[77] falsely what they see aright?
If that be fair whereon my false eyes dote,
    What means the world to say it is not so?
If it be not, then love doth well denote
    Love's eye is not so true as all men's: no.
How can it? O how can Love's eye be true,
    That is so vex'd with watching and with tears?
No marvel then though I mistake my view;
    The sun itself sees not, till heaven clears.
        O cunning Love! with tears thou keep'st me
           blind,
        Lest eyes well-seeing thy foul faults should find.

CXLIX

Canst thou, O cruel! say I love thee not,
    When I, against myself, with thee partake?[78]
Do I not think on thee, when I forgot
    Am of myself, all tyrant, for thy sake?
Who hateth thee that I do call my friend?
    On whom frown'st thou that I do fawn upon?
Nay if thou low'rst on me, do I not spend
    Revenge upon myself with present moan?
What merit do I in myself respect,
    That is so proud thy service to despise,
When all my best doth worship thy defect,
    Commanded by the motion of thine eyes?
        But, love, hate on, for now I know thy mind;
        Those that can see thou lov'st, and I am blind.

77 *censures*] i. e. estimates.
78 *partake*] i. e. take part.

127

CL

O, from what power hast thou this powerful might,
  With insufficiency my heart to sway?
To make me give the lie to my true sight,
  And swear that brightness doth not grace the day?
Whence hast thou this becoming of things ill,
  That in the very refuse of thy deeds
There is such strength and warrantise of skill,
  That in my mind, thy worst all best exceeds?
Who taught thee how to make me love thee more,
  The more I hear and see just cause of hate?
O, though I love what others do abhor,
    With others thou should'st not abhor my state;
      If thy unworthiness rais'd love in me,
      More worthy I to be belov'd of thee.

CLI

Love is too young to know what conscience is;
  Yet who knows not, conscience is born of love?
Then, gentle cheater, urge not my amiss,[79]
  Lest guilty of my faults thy sweet self prove.
For thou betraying me, I do betray
  My nobler part to my gross body's treason;
My soul doth tell my body that he may
  Triumph in love; flesh stays no farther reason;
But rising at thy name, doth point out thee
  As his triumphant prize. Proud of this pride,
He is contented thy poor drudge to be,
  To stand in thy affairs, fall by thy side.
    No want of conscience hold it that I call
    Her—love, for whose dear love I rise and fall.

[79] *amiss*] i. e. fault.

128

CLII

In loving thee thou know'st I am forsworn,
But thou art twice forsworn, to me love swearing;
In act thy bed-vow broke, and new faith torn,
In vowing new hate after new love bearing.
But why of two oaths' breach do I accuse thee,
When I break twenty? I am perjur'd most;
For all my vows were oaths but to misuse thee,
And all my honest faith in thee is lost:
For I have sworn deep oaths of thy deep kindness,
Oaths of thy love, thy truth, thy constancy;
And, to enlighten thee, gave eyes to blindness,
Or made them swear against the thing they see;
For I have sworn thee fair: more perjur'd I,
To swear, against the truth, so foul a lie!

CLIII

Cupid laid by his brand, and fell asleep:
A maid of Dian's this advantage found,
And his love-kindling fire did quickly steep
In a cold valley-fountain of that ground;
Which borrow'd from this holy fire of love
A dateless lively heat, still to endure,
And grew a seething bath, which yet men prove
Against strange maladies a soverign cure.
But at my mistress' eye love's brand new-fir'd,
The boy for trial needs would touch my breast;
I sick withal, the help of bath desir'd,
And thither hied, a sad distemper'd guest,
But found no cure; the bath for my help lies
Where Cupid got new fire; my mistress' eyes.

129

CLIV

The little love-god lying once asleep,
   Laid by his side his heart-inflaming brand,
Whilst many nymphs that vow'd chaste life to keep,
   Came tripping by; but in her maiden hand
The fairest votary took up that fire
   Which many legions of true hearts had warm'd;
And so the general of hot desire
   Was sleeping by a virgin hand disarm'd.
This brand she quenched in a cool well by,
   Which from love's fire took heat perpetual,
Growing a bath and healthful remedy
   For men diseas'd; but I, my mistress' thrall,
      Came there for cure, and this by that I prove,
      Love's fire heats water, water cools not love.

A LOVER'S COMPLAINT

A LOVER'S
COMPLAINT

FROM OFF A HILL WHOSE CONCAVE
WOMB RE-WORDED
A PLAINTFUL STORY FROM A
SISTERING VALE,

My spirits to attend this double voice accorded
  And down I lay to list the sad-tun'd tale:
  Ere long espy'd a fickle maid full pale,
    Tearing of papers, breaking rings a-twain,
    Storming her world with sorrow's wind and rain.

Upon her head a platted hive of straw,
  Which fortified her visage from the sun,
Whereon the thought might think sometime it saw
  The carcase of a beauty spent and done.
  Time had not scythed all that youth begun,
    Nor youth all quit; but, spite of heaven's fell rage,
    Some beauty peep'd through lattice of sear'd age.

Oft did she heave her napkin to her eyne,
  Which on it had conceited[1] characters,
Laund'ring[2] the silken figures in the brine
  That season'd woe had pelleted[3] in tears,
  And often reading what contents it bears;
    As often shrieking undistinguish'd woe,
    In clamours of all size, both high and low.

Sometimes her levell'd[4] eyes their carriage ride,
  As they did battery to the spheres intend;
Sometime diverted their poor balls are ty'd
  To the orb'd earth: sometimes they do extend
  To view right on; anon their gazes lend
    To every place at once, and no where fix'd,
    The mind and sight distractedly commix'd.

Her hair, nor loose, nor ty'd in formal plat,
  Proclaim'd in her a careless hand of pride;

[1] *conceited*] i. e. fanciful.
[2] *laund'ring*] i. e. washing.
[3] *pelleted*] i. e. made into pellets, balls.
[4] *levell'd eyes*, &c.] An allusion to a piece of ordnance.

For some, untuck'd, descended her sheav'd⁵ hat,
　　Hanging her pale and pined cheek beside;
Some in her threaden fillet still did bide,
　　And, true to bondage, would not break from
　　　　thence,
　　　Though slackly braided in loose negligence.

A thousand favours from a maund⁶ she drew
　　Of amber, crystal, and of beaded jet,
Which one by one she in a river threw,
　　Upon whose weeping margent she was set;
　　Like usury, applying wet to wet,
　　　Or monarch's hands, that let no bounty fall
　　　Where want cries *some,* but where excess begs
　　　　all.

Of folded schedules had she many a one,
　　Which she perus'd, sigh'd, tore, and gave the flood;
Crack'd many a ring of posied gold and bone,
　　Bidding them find their sepulchres in mud;
　　Found yet more letters sadly penn'd in blood,
　　　With sleided⁷ silk feat⁸ and affectedly
　　　Enswath'd, and seal'd to curious secrecy.

These often bath'd she in her fluxive eyes,
　　And often kiss'd, and often 'gan⁹ to tear;
Cried, "O false blood! thou register of lies,
　　"What unapproved witness dost thou bear!
　　"Ink would have seem'd more black and damned
　　　here!"
　　　This said, in top of rage the lines she rents,
　　　Big discontent so breaking their contents.

⁵ *sheav'd*] i. e. straw.
⁶ *maund*] i. e. hand basket.
⁷ *sleided*] i. e. raw, untwisted.
⁸ *feat*] i. e. neatly, curiously.
⁹ *'gan*] Malone's conjecture for "gave."

A reverend man that graz'd his cattle nigh,
    Sometime a blusterer, that the ruffle knew
Of court, of city, and had let go by
    The swiftest hours, observed as they flew;
    Towards this afflicted fancy[10] fastly drew;
        And, privileg'd by age, desires to know
        In brief, the grounds and motives of her woe.

So slides he down upon his grained bat,[11]
    And comely-distant sits he by her side;
When he again desires her, being sat,
    Her grievance with his hearing to divide:
    If that from him there may be aught applied
        Which may her suffering ecstasy assuage,
        'Tis promis'd in the charity of age.

"Father," she says, "though in me you behold
    "The injury of many a blasting hour,
"Let it not tell your judgment I am old;
    "Not age, but sorrow, over me hath power:
    "I might as yet have been a spreading flower,
        "Fresh to myself, if I had self-applied
        "Love to myself, and to no love beside.

"But woe is me! too early I attended
    "A youthful suit (it was to gain my grace)
"Of one by nature's outwards so commended,
    "That maiden's eyes stuck over all his face:
    "Love lack'd a dwelling, and made him her place;
        "And when in his fair parts she did abide,
        "She was new lodg'd, and newly deified.

"His browny locks did hang in crooked curls;
    "And every light occasion of the wind

10 *fancy*] i. e. enamoured one: *fancy* occurs several times in this vol. in
the sense of love.   11 *bat*] i. e. club.

"Upon his lips their silken parcels hurls.
　"What's sweet to do, to do will aptly find:
　"Each eye that saw him did enchant the mind;
　　"For on his visage was in little drawn,
　　"What largeness thinks in paradise was sawn.[12]

"Small show of man was yet upon his chin;
　"His phœnix down began but to appear,
"Like unshorn velvet, on that termless skin,
　　"Whose bare out-bragg'd the web it seem'd to wear;
　　"Yet show'd his visage by that cost most dear;
　　　"And nice affections wavering stood in doubt
　　　"If best 'twere as it was, or best without.

"His qualities were beauteous as his form,
　"For maiden-tongued he was, and thereof free;
"Yet, if men mov'd him, was he such a storm
　　"As oft 'twixt May and April is to see,
　　"When winds breathe sweet, unruly though they be.
　　　"His rudeness so with his authoriz'd youth,
　　　"Did livery falseness in a pride of truth.

"Well could he ride, and often men would say
　　"*That horse his mettle from his rider takes:*
"*Proud of subjection, noble by the sway,*
　　"*What rounds, what bounds, what course, what stop
　　　　he makes!*
　　"And controversy hence a question takes,
　　　"Whether the horse by him became his deed,
　　　"Or he his manage by the well-doing steed.

"But quickly on this side the verdict went;
　"His real habitude gave life and grace

12 *sawn*] i. e. sown.

"To appertainings and to ornament,
 "Accomplish'd in himself, not in his case:
 "All aids, themselves made fairer by their place,
  "Came for additions; yet their purpos'd trim
  "Piec'd not his grace, but were all grac'd by him.

"So on the tip of his subduing tongue
 "All kind of arguments and question deep,
"All replication prompt, and reason strong,
 "For his advantage still did wake and sleep:
 "To make the weeper laugh, the laugher weep,
  "He had the dialect and different skill,
  "Catching all passions in his craft of will;

"That he did in the general bosom reign
 "Of young, of old; and sexes both enchanted,
"To dwell with him in thoughts, or to remain
 "In personal duty, following where he haunted:
 "Consents bewitch'd, ere he desire, have granted;
  "And dialogu'd for him what he would say,
  "Ask'd their own wills, and made their wills
     obey.

"Many there were that did his picture get,
 "To serve their eyes, and in it put their mind;
"Like fools that in the imagination set
 "The goodly objects which abroad they find
 "Of lands and mansions, their's in thought assign'd;
  "And laboring in more pleasures to bestow them,
  "Than the true gouty landlord which doth owe[13]
     them:

"So many have, that never touch'd his hand,
 "Sweetly suppos'd them mistress of his heart.

13 *owe*] i. e. own.

139

"My woeful self, that did in freedom stand,
  "And was my own fee-simple, (not in part,)
"What with his art in youth, and youth in art,
    "Threw my affections in his charmed power,
    "Reserv'd the stalk, and gave him all my flower.

"Yet did I not, as some my equals did,
  "Demand of him, nor being desired, yielded;
"Finding myself in honour so forbid,
  "With safest distance I mine honour shielded:
  "Experience for me many bulwarks builded
    "Of proofs new-bleeding, which remain'd the foil
    "Of this false jewel, and his amorous spoil.

"But ah! who ever shunn'd by precedent
  "The destin'd ill she must herself assay?
"Or forc'd examples, 'gainst her own content,
  "To put the by-pass'd perils in her way?
  "Counsel may stop a while what will not stay;
    "For when we rage, advice is often seen
    "By blunting us to make our wits more keen.

"Nor gives it satisfaction to our blood,
  "That we must curb it upon others' proof,
"To be forbid the sweets that seem so good,
  "For fear of harms that preach in our behoof.
  "O appetite, from judgment stand aloof!
    "The one a palate hath that needs will taste,
    "Though reason weep, and cry *it is thy last.*

"For further I could say, *this man's untrue,*
  "And knew the patterns of his foul beguiling;
"Heard where his plants in others' orchards grew,

"Saw how deceits were gilded in his smiling;
"Knew vows were ever brokers[14] to defiling;
  "Thought, characters, and words, merely but art,
  "And bastards of his foul adulterate heart.

"And long upon these terms I held my city,
  "Till thus he 'gan besiege me: *Gentle maid,*
"Have of my suffering youth some feeling pity,
  "And be not of my holy vows afraid:
  "That's to you sworn, to none was ever said;
    "For feasts of love I have been call'd unto,
    "Till now did ne'er invite, nor never vow.

"All my offences that abroad you see,
  "Are errors of the blood, none of the mind;
"Love made them not; with acture[15] they may be,
  "Where neither party is nor true nor kind:
  "They sought their shame that so their shame did
      find;
    "And so much less of shame in me remains,
    "By how much of me their reproach contains.

"Among the many that mine eyes have seen,
  "Not one whose flame my heart so much as warm'd,
"Or my affection put to the smallest teen,[16]
  "Or any of my leisures ever charm'd:
  "Harm have I done to them, but ne'er was harm'd;
    "Kept hearts in liveries, but mine own was free,
    "And reign'd, commanding in his monarchy.

"Look here what tributes wounded fancies[17] sent me,
  "Of paled pearls, and rubies red as blood;
"Figuring that they their passions likewise lent me

14 *brokers*] i. e. pandars.   16 *teen*] i. e. grief.
15 *acture*] i. e. action.   17 *fancies*] See note 10 above.

"Of grief and blushes, aptly understood
"In bloodless white and the encrimson'd mood;
  "Effects of terror and dear modesty,
  "Encamp'd in hearts, but fighting outwardly.

"And lo! behold these talents of their hair,[18]
  "With twisted metal amorously impleach'd,[19]
"I have receiv'd from many a several fair,
  "(Their kind acceptance weepingly beseech'd,)
  "With the annexions of fair gems enrich'd,
    "And deep-brain'd sonnets that did amplify
    "Each stone's dear nature, worth, and quality.

"The diamond; why 'twas beautiful and hard,
  "Whereto his invis'd[20] properties did tend;
"The deep-green emerald, in whose fresh regard
  "Weak sights their sickly radiance do amend;
  "The heaven-hued sapphire and the opal blend
    "With objects manifold; each several stone,
    "With wit well blazon'd, smil'd or made some
      moan.

"Lo! all these trophies of affections hot,
  "Of pensiv'd and subdued desires the tender,
"Nature hath charg'd me that I hoard them not,
  "But yield them up where I myself must render,
  "That is, to you, my origin and ender:
    "For these, of force, must your oblations be,
    "Since I their altar, you enpatron me.

"O then advance of yours that phraseless hand,
  "Whose white weighs down the airy scale of praise;

18 *talents of their hair*, &c.] i. e. "lockets, consisting of hair platted and set
in gold." MALONE.
19 *impleach'd*] i. e. interwoven.   20 *invis'd*] i. e. invisible.

142

"*Take all these similes to your own command,*
   "*Hallow'd with sighs that burning lungs did raise;*
   "*What me your minister, for you obeys,*
     "*Works under you; and to your audit comes*
     "*Their distract parcels in combined sums.*

"*Lo! this device was sent me from a nun,*
   "*Or sister sanctified of holiest note;*
"*Which late her noble suit*²¹ *in court did shun,*
   "*Whose rarest havings made the blossoms dote;*²²
"*For she was sought by spirits of richest coat,*²³
     "*But kept cold distance, and did thence remove,*
     "*To spend her living in eternal love.*

"*But O, my sweet, what labour is't to leave*
   "*The thing we have not, mastering what not strives?*
"*Playing the place which did no form receive,*
   "*Playing patient sports in unconstrained gyves:*
"*She that her fame so to herself contrives,*
     "*The scars of battle 'scapeth by the flight,*
     "*And makes her absence valiant, not her might.*

"*O pardon me, in that my boast is true;*
   "*The accident which brought me to her eye,*
"*Upon the moment did her force subdue,*
   "*And now she would the caged cloister fly:*
   "*Religious love put out religion's eye:*
     "*Not to be tempted, would she be immur'd,*
     "*And now, to tempt all, liberty procur'd.*

²¹ *suit*] i. e. suitors.
²² *Whose rarest havings made the blossoms dote*] "Whose accomplishments were so extraordinary, that the flower of the young nobility were passionately enamoured of her." MALONE. It may be doubted, however, if *"havings"* is not used here in its usual sense of *fortune, estate,* and not in that of *accomplishments.*
²³ *coat*] i. e. coat of arms.

"How mighty then you are, O hear me tell!
"The broken bosoms that to me belong,
"Have emptied all their fountains in my well,
"And mine I pour your ocean all among:
"I strong o'er them, and you o'er me being strong,
"Must for your victory us all congest,
"As compound love to physick your cold breast.

"My parts had power to charm a sacred nun,
"Who disciplin'd and dieted in grace,
"Believ'd her eyes when they to assail begun,
"All vows and consecrations giving place.
"O most potential love! vow, bond, nor space,
"In thee hath neither sting, knot, nor confine,
"For thou art all, and all things else are thine.

"When thou impressest, what are precepts worth
"Of stale example? When thou wilt inflame,
"How coldly those impediments stand forth
"Of wealth, of filial fear, law, kindred, fame?
"Love's arms are peace, 'gainst rule, 'gainst sense,
   'gainst shame,
"And sweetens, in the suffering pangs it bears,
"The aloes of all forces, shocks, and fears.

"Now all these hearts that do on mine depend,
"Feeling it break, with bleeding groans they pine,
"And supplicant their sighs to you extend,
"To leave the battery that you make 'gainst mine,
"Lending soft audience to my sweet design,
"And credent soul to that strongbonded oath,
"That shall prefer and undertake my troth.

"This said, his watery eyes[27] he did dismount,
 "Whose sights till then were levell'd on my face;
"Each cheek a river running from a fount
 "With brinish current downward flow'd apace:
 "O how the channel to the stream gave grace!
  "Who, glaz'd with crystal, gate[28] the glowing
   roses
  "That flame through water which their hue
   incloses.

"O father, what a hell of witchcraft lies
 "In the small orb of one particular tear?
"But with the inundation of the eyes
 "What rocky heart to water will not wear?
 "What breast so cold that is not warmed here?
  "O cleft effect! cold modesty, hot wrath,
  "Both fire from hence and chill extincture hath!

"For lo! his passion, but an art of craft,
 "Even there resolv'd my reason into tears;
"There my white stole of chastity I daff'd,
 "Shook off my sober guards, and civil[29] fears;
 "Appear to him, as he to me appears,
  "All melting; though our drops this difference
   bore,
  "His poison'd me, and mine did him restore.

"In him a plenitude of subtle matter,
 "Applied to cautels,[30] all strange forms receives,
"Of burning blushes, or of weeping water,

27 *his watery eyes,* &c.] "The allusion is to the old English fire-arms, which were supported on what was called a *rest.*" MALONE.
28 *gate*] i. e. got.
29 *civil*] i. e. grave.
30 *cautels*] i. e. deceits, insidious purposes.

"Or swooning paleness; and he takes and leaves,
"In either's aptness, as it best deceives,
  "To blush at speeches rank, to weep at woes,
  "Or to turn white and swoon at tragick shows;

"That not a heart which in his level came,
  "Could scape the hail of his all-hurting aim,
"Showing fair nature is both kind and tame;
  "And veil'd in them, did win whom he would
     maim:
  "Against the thing he sought he would exclaim;
    "When he most burn'd in heart-wish'd luxury,[31]
    "He preach'd pure maid, and prais'd cold
     chastity.

"Thus merely with the garment of a Grace
  "The naked and concealed fiend he cover'd,
"That the unexperienc'd gave the tempter place,
  "Which, like a cherubin, above them hover'd.
  "Who, young and simple, would not be so lover'd?
    "Ah me! I fell; and yet do question make
    "What I should do again for such a sake.

"O, that infected moisture of his eye,
  "O, that false fire which in his cheek so glow'd,
"O, that forc'd thunder from his heart did fly,
  "O, that sad breath his spungy lungs bestow'd,
  "O, all that borrow'd motion, seeming ow'd,[32]
    "Would yet again betray the fore-betray'd,
    "And new pervert a reconciled maid!"

31 *luxury*] i. e. lewdness.
32 *ow'd*] i. e. owned, his own.

THE PASSIONATE
PILGRIM

PASSIONATE

PILGRIM

WHEN MY LOVE SWEARS THAT SHE IS
      MADE OF TRUTH,
   I DO BELIEVE HER, THOUGH I KNOW
      SHE LIES,
THAT SHE MIGHT THINK ME SOME
      UNTUTOR'D YOUTH,
   UNSKILFUL IN THE WORLD'S FALSE
      FORGERIES.

150

Thus vainly thinking that she thinks me young,
    Although I know my years be past the best,
I smiling credit her false-speaking tongue,
    Outfacing faults in love with love's ill rest.
But wherefore says my love that she is young?
    And wherefore say not I that I am old?
O, love's best habit is a soothing tongue,
    And age, in love, loves not to have years told.
        Therefore I'll lie with love, and love with me,
        Since that our faults in love thus smother'd be.

II

Two loves I have, of comfort and despair,
    That like two spirits do suggest me still;
My better angel is a man right fair,
    My worser spirit a woman colour'd ill.
To win me soon to hell, my female evil
    Tempteth my better angel from my side,
And would corrupt my saint to be a devil,
    Wooing his purity with her fair pride.
And whether that my angel be turn'd fiend,
    Suspect I may, yet not directly tell:
For being both to me, both to each friend,
    I guess one angel in another's hell:
        The truth I shall not know, but live in doubt,
        Till my bad angel fire my good one out.

III

Did not the heavenly rhetoric of thine eye,
    'Gainst whom the world could not hold argument,
Persuade my heart to this false perjury?
    Vows for thee broke deserve not punishment.
A woman I forswore; but I will prove,
    Thou being a goddess, I forswore not thee:
My vow was earthly, thou a heavenly love:

151

Thy grace being gain'd cures all disgrace in me.
My vow was breath, and breath a vapour is;
   Then, thou fair sun, that on this earth doth shine,
Exhale this vapour vow; in thee it is:
   If broken, then it is no fault of mine.
      If by me broke, what fool is not so wise
      To break an oath, to win a paradise?

IV

Sweet Cytherea, sitting by a brook
   With young Adonis, lovely, fresh and green,
Did court the lad with many a lovely look,
   Such looks as none could look but beauty's queen.
She told him stories to delight his ear,
   She show'd him favours to allure his eye;
To win his heart, she touch'd him here and there;
   Touches so soft still conquer chastity.
But whether unripe years did want conceit,
   Or he refused to take her figured proffer,
The tender nibbler would not touch the bait,
   But smile, and jest at every gentle offer:
      Then fell she on her back, fair queen, and
         toward:
      He rose and ran away; ah, fool too froward.

V

If love make me forsworn, how shall I swear to love?
   O never faith could hold, if not to beauty vowed:
Though to myself forsworn, to thee I'll constant prove:
   Those thoughts, to me like oaks, to thee like osiers
         bowed.
Study his bias leaves, and make his book thine eyes,
   Where all those pleasures live that art can
         comprehend.

If knowledge be the mark, to know thee shall suffice;
  Well learned is that tongue that well can thee
      commend:
All ignorant that soul that sees thee without wonder;
  Which is to me some praise, that I thy parts
      admire:
Thine eye Jove's lightning seems, thy voice his dread-
      ful thunder,
  Which, not to anger bent, is music and sweet fire.
    Celestial as thou art, O do not love that wrong,
     To sing heaven's praise with such an earthly
      tongue.

VI

Scarce had the sun dried up the dewy morn,
  And scarce the herd gone to the hedge for shade,
When Cytherea, all in love forlorn,
  A longing tarriance for Adonis made
Under an osier growing by a brook,
  A brook where Adon used to cool his spleen:
Hot was the day; she hotter that did look
  For his approach, that often there had been.
Anon he comes, and throws his mantle by,
  And stood stark naked on the brook's green brim:
The sun look'd on the world with glorious eye,
  Yet not so wistly as this queen on him.
    He, spying her, bounced in, whereas he stood:
    "O Jove," quoth she, "why was not I a flood!"

VII

Fair is my love, but not so fair as fickle,
  Mild as a dove, but neither true or trusty,
Brighter than glass and yet, as glass is, brittle,
  Softer than wax and yet as iron rusty:

153

A lily pale, with damask dye to grace her,
None fairer, nor none falser to deface her.

Her lips to mine how often hath she joined,
    Between each kiss her oaths of true love swearing!
How many tales to please me hath she coined,
    Dreading my love, the loss thereof still fearing!
        Yet in the midst of all her pure protestings,
        Her faith, her oaths, her tears, and all were
        jestings.

She burn'd with love, as straw with fire flameth;
    She burn'd out love, as soon as straw out-burneth;
She framed the love, and yet she foil'd the framing;
    She bade love last, and yet she fell a-turning.
        Was this a lover, or a lecher whether?
        Bad in the best, though excellent in neither.

VIII

If music and sweet poetry agree,
    As they must needs, the sister and the brother,
Then must the love be great 'twixt thee and me,
    Because thou lovest the one and I the other.
Dowland to thee is dear, whose heavenly touch
    Upon the lute doth ravish human sense;
Spenser to me, whose deep conceit is such
    As passing all conceit needs no defence.
Thou lovest to hear the sweet melodious sound
    That Phoebus' lute, the queen of music, makes;
And I in deep delight am chiefly drown'd
    When as himself to singing he betakes.
        One god is god of both, as poets feign;
        One knight loves both, and both in thee remain.

154

IX

Fair was the morn when the fair queen of love,
[Here a line is missing in the original]
Paler for sorrow than her milk-white dove,
    For Adon's sake, a youngster proud and wild;
Her stand she takes upon a steep-up hill:
    Anon Adonis comes with horn and hounds;
She, silly queen, with more than love's good will,
    Forbade the boy he should not pass those grounds:
"Once," quoth she, "did I see a fair sweet youth
    "Here in these brakes deep-wounded with a boar,
"Deep in the thigh, a spectacle of ruth!
    "See, in my thigh," quoth she, "here was the sore."
        She showed hers: he saw more wounds than one,
        And blushing fled, and left her all alone.

X

Sweet rose, fair flower, untimely pluck'd, soon vaded,
    Pluck'd in the bud and vaded in the spring!
Bright orient pearl, alack, too timely shaded!
    Fair creature, kill'd too soon by death's sharp sting!
        Like a green plum that hangs upon a tree,
        And falls through wind before the fall
          should be.

I weep for thee and yet no cause I have;
    For why thou left'st me nothing in thy will:
And yet thou left'st me more than I did crave;
    For why I craved nothing of thee still:
        Oh yes, dear friend, I pardon crave of thee,
        Thy discontent thou didst bequeath to me.

XI

Venus, with young Adonis sitting by her
    Under a myrtle shade, began to woo him:

She told the youngling how god Mars did try her,
    And as he fell to her, so fell she to him,
"Even thus," quoth she, "the warlike god embraced
    me,"
    And then she clipp'd Adonis in her arms;
"Even thus," quoth she, "the warlike god unlaced me,"
    As if the boy should use like loving charms;

"Even thus," quoth she, "he seized on my lips,"
    And with her lips on his did act the seizure:
And as she fetched breath, away he skips,
    And would not take her meaning nor her pleasure.
    Ah, that I had my lady at this bay,
    To kiss and clip me till I run away!

XII

Crabbed age and youth cannot live together:
 Youth is full of pleasance, age is full of care;
Youth like summer morn, age like winter weather;
 Youth like summer brave, age like winter bare.
Youth is full of sport, age's breath is short;
 Youth is nimble, age is lame;
Youth is hot and bold, age is weak and cold;
 Youth is wild, and age is tame.
Age, I do abhor thee; youth, I do adore thee;
 O, my love, my love is young!
Age, I do defy thee: O, sweet shepherd, hie thee,
 For methinks thou stay'st too long.

XIII

Beauty is but a vain and doubtful good;
 A shining gloss that vadeth suddenly;
A flower that dies when first it 'gins to bud;
 A brittle glass that's broken presently:
  A doubtful good, a gloss, a glass, a flower,
  Lost, vaded, broken, dead within an hour.
And as goods lost are seld or never found,
 As vaded gloss no rubbing will refresh,
As flowers dead lie wither'd on the ground,
 As broken glass no cement can redress,
  So beauty blemish'd once's for ever lost,
  In spite of physic, painting, pain and cost.

XIV

Good night, good rest. Ah, neither be my share:
 She bade good night that kept my rest away;
And daff'd me to a cabin hang'd with care,
 To descant on the doubts of my decay.

157

"Farewell," quoth she, "and come again
    tomorrow":
Fare well I could not, for I supp'd with sorrow.

Yet at my parting sweetly did she smile,
    In scorn or friendship, nill I construe whether:
'T may be, she joy'd to jest at my exile,
    'T may be, again to make me wander thither:
        "Wander," a word for shadows like myself,
        As take the pain, but cannot pluck the pelf.

XV

Lord, how mine eyes throw gazes to the east!
    My heart doth charge the watch; the morning rise
Doth cite each moving sense from idle rest.
    Not daring trust the office of mine eyes,
        While Philomena sits and sings, I sit and mark,
        And wish her lays were tuned like the lark;

For she doth welcome daylight with her ditty,
    And drives away dark dreaming night:
The night so pack'd, I post unto my pretty;
    Heart hath his hope and eyes their wished sight;
        Sorrow changed to solace and solace mixed with
            sorrow;
        For why, she sigh'd, and bade me come
            tomorrow.

Were I with her, the night would post too soon;
    But now are minutes added to the hours;
To spite me now, each minute seems a moon;
    Yet not for me, shine sun to succour flowers!

158

Pack night, peep day; good day, of night now
    borrow:
Short, night, to-night, and length thyself
    tomorrow.

XVI

It was a lording's daughter, the fairest one of three,
That liked of her master as well as well might be,
Till looking on an Englishman, the fair'st that eye
        could see,
    Her fancy fell a-turning.
Long was the combat doubtful that love with love did
        fight,
To leave the master loveless, or kill the gallant knight:
To put in practice either, alas, it was a spite
    Unto the silly damsel!
But one must be refused; more mickle was the pain
That nothing could be used to turn them both to gain,
For of the two the trusty knight was wounded with
        disdain:
    Alas, she could not help it!
Thus art with arms contending was victor of the day,
Which by a gift of learning did bear the maid away:
Then, lullaby, the learned man hath got the lady gay;
    For now my song is ended.

XVII

On a day, alack the day!
Love, whose month was ever May,
    Spied a blossom passing fair,
    Playing in the wanton air:
        Through the velvet leaves the wind
        All unseen 'gan passage find;

159

That the lover, sick to death,
Wish'd himself the heaven's breath,
   "Air," quoth he, "thy cheeks may blow;
   Air, would I might triumph so!
      But, alas! my hand hath sworn
      Ne'er to pluck thee from thy thorn:
Vow, alack! for youth unmeet:
Youth, so apt to pluck a sweet.
   Thou for whom Jove would swear
   Juno but an Ethiope were;
      And deny himself for Jove,
      Turning mortal for thy love."

XVIII

My flocks feed not,
  My ewes breed not,
    My rams speed not;
      All is amiss:
Love's denying,
  Faith's defying,
    Heart's renying
      Causer of this.
All my merry jigs are quite forgot,
All my lady's love is lost, God wot:
   Where her faith was firmly fix'd in love,
   There a nay is placed without remove.
One silly cross
Wrought all my loss;
      O frowning Fortune, cursed, fickle dame!
For now I see
Inconstancy
      More in women than in men remain.

In black mourn I,
  All fears scorn I,

160

Love hath forlorn me
  Living in thrall;
Heart is bleeding,
 All help needing,
  O cruel speeding,
   Fraughted with gall.
My shepherd's pipe can sound no deal:
My wether's bell rings doleful knell;
 My curtal dog, that wont to have play'd,
 Plays not at all, but seems afraid;
My sighs so deep
Procure to weep,
  In howling wise, to see my doleful plight.
How sighs resound
Through heartless ground,
  Like a thousand vanquish'd men in bloody
   fight!

Clear wells spring not,
 Sweet birds sing not,
  Green plants bring not
   Forth their dye;
Herds stand weeping,
 Flocks all sleeping,
  Nymphs back peeping
   Fearfully:
All our pleasure known to us poor swains,
All our merry meetings on the plains,
 All our evening sport from us is fled,
 All our love is lost, for Love is dead.
Farewell, sweet lass,
They like ne'er was
  For a sweet content, the cause of all my moan:

Poor Corydon
Must live alone;
       Other help for him I see that there is none.

XIX

When as thine eye hath chose the dame,
  And stall'd the deer that thou shouldst strike,
Let reason rule things worthy blame,
  As well as fancy, partial wight:
    Take counsel of some wiser head,
    Neither too young nor yet unwed.

And when thou comest thy tale to tell,
  Smooth not thy tongue with filed talk,
Let she some subtle practice smell,—
  A cripple soon can find a halt;—
    But plainly say thou lovest her well,
    And set thy person forth to sell.

What though her frowning brows be bent,
  Her cloudy looks will calm ere night:
And then too late she will repent
  That thus dissembled her delight;
    And twice desire, ere it be day,
    That which with scorn she put away.

What though her frowning brows be bent,
  And ban and brawl, and say thee nay,
Her feeble force will yield at length,
  When craft hath taught her thus to say;
    "Had women been so strong as men,
    "In faith, you had not had it then."

And to her will frame all thy ways;
  Spare not to spend, and chiefly there

Where thy desert may merit praise,
    By ringing in thy lady's ear:
        The strongest castle, tower and town,
        The golden bullet beats it down.

Serve always with assured trust,
    And in thy suit be humble true;
Unless thy lady prove unjust,
    Press never thou to choose anew:
        When time shall serve, be thou not slack
        To proffer, though she put thee back.

The wiles and guiles that women work,
    Dissembled with an outward show,
The tricks and toys that in them lurk,
    The cock that treads them shall not know.
        Have you not heard it said full oft,
        A woman's nay doth stand for nought?

Think women still to strive with men,
    To sin and never for to saint:
There is no heaven, by holy then,
    When time with age shall them attaint.
        Were kisses all the joys in bed,
        One woman would another wed.

But, soft! enough—too much, I fear—
    Lest that my mistress hear my song:
She will not stick to round me on th' ear,
    To teach my tongue to be so long:
        Yet will she blush, here be it said,
        To hear her secrets so bewray'd.

XX

Live with me, and be my love,
    And we will all the pleasures prove

163

That hills and valleys, dales and fields,
　And all the craggy mountains yields.
There will we sit upon the rocks,
　And see the shepherds feed their flocks,
　　By shallow rivers, by whose falls
　　　Melodious birds sing madrigals.
There will I make thee a bed of roses,
　With a thousand fragrant posies,
　　A cap of flowers, and a kirtle
　　　Embroider'd all with leaves of myrtle.
A belt of straw and ivy buds,
　With coral clasps and amber studs;
　　And if these pleasures may thee move,
　　　Then live with me and be my love.

LOVE'S ANSWER

If that the world and love were young,
　And truth in every shepherd's tongue,
　　These pretty pleasures might me move
　　　To live with thee and be thy love.

XXI

As it fell upon a day
In the merry month of May,
　Sitting in a pleasant shade
　Which a grove of myrtles made,
　　Beasts did leap and birds did sing,
　　Trees did grow and plants did spring;
Every thing did banish moan,
Save the nightingale alone:
　She, poor bird, as all forlorn,
　Lean'd her breast up-till a thorn,

164

And there sung the dolefull'st ditty,
That to hear it was great pity:
"Fie, fie, fie," now would she cry;
"Tereu, Tereu!" by and by;
That to hear her so complain,
Scarce I could from tears refrain;
For her griefs so lively shown
Made me think upon mine own.

Ah, thought I, thou mourn'st in vain!
None takes pity on thy pain:
Senseless trees they cannot hear thee;
Ruthless beasts they will not cheer thee:
King Pandion he is dead;
All thy friends are lapp'd in lead;
All thy fellow birds do sing,
Careless of thy sorrowing.
Even so, poor bird, like thee,
None alive will pity me.
Whilst as fickle Fortune smiled,
Thou and I were both beguiled.
Every one that flatters thee
Is no friend in misery.
Words are easy, like the wind;
Faithful friends are hard to find:
Every man will be thy friend
Whilst thou hast wherewith to spend;
But if store of crowns be scant,
No man will supply thy want.
If that one be prodigal,
Bountiful they will him call,
And with such-like flattering,
"Pity but he were a king";

165

If he be addict to vice,
Quickly him they will entice;
   If to women he be bent,
   They have at commandment:
      But if Fortune once do frown,
      Then farewell his great renown;
They that fawn'd on him before
Use his company no more.
   He that is thy friend indeed,
   He will help thee in thy need:
      If thou sorrow, he will weep;
      If thou wake, he cannot sleep;
Thus of every grief in heart
He with thee doth bear a part.
   These are certain signs to know
   Faithful friend from flattering foe.